D1242313

The
Fountain Pen
A Collector's Companion

The
Fountain Pen
A Collector's Companion

ALEXANDER CRUM EWING

AN IMPRINT OF RUNNING PRESS
PHILADELPHIA · LONDON

A QUINTET BOOK

9 8 7 6 5 4 3 2 1

Digit on the right indicates the number
of this printing

ISBN 0-7624-0008-0

Library of Congress
Cataloging-in-Publication Number
96-69262

This book was designed and produced by
Quintet Publishing Limited
The Old Brewery
6 Blundell Street
London N7 9BH

Creative Director: Richard Dewing
Designer: Ian Hunt
Senior Editor: Anna Briffa
Editor: Anna Bennett
Photographer: Keith Waterton

Typeset in Great Britain by
Central Southern Typesetters, Eastbourne
Manufactured in Singapore by Bright Arts Pte Ltd
Printed in China by Leefung-Asco Printers Ltd

Running Press Book Publishers
125 South Twenty-second Street
Philadelphia, Pennsylvania 19103-4399

Contents

Foreword

THE FOUNTAIN PEN IS currently enjoying a renaissance as a writing instrument, a fashion statement, a collector's item and even as an investment. Today there is an almost bewildering array of fountain pens for sale, supplied by a range of manufacturers greater than at any time since the 1920s. We are able to choose from restyled lines of the international brands, from almost forgotten companies now dusted down and rejuvenated, and from the innovative designs of independent companies that have sprung up in the last decade.

The first section of this book *The Story of the Fountain Pen* covers the story of the "fountain pen before the fountain pen" for the first time in a major book. In *The Fountain Pen Directory* section, Alexander Crum Ewing guides us through the world's leading quality fountain pen brands and their ever-widening range of pens in an authorative and informative fashion. Such a work on this subject has been long overdue and I for one am delighted that contemporary pens have finally received the attention in print that they so richly deserve.

DR DIGBY LOWWE-SANDES
Clifton, Bristol, August 1996.

Author's Acknowledgements

It would not have been possible to write this book without the help of my colleagues at Bonhams, in particular Sara Sturgess, Elizabeth Carr Wilson, Nicola Tonkinson, Georgina Whiteman, James Hammond, and members of the photographic department past and present whose work is reproduced here, including Simon Bevan, Sue Barr, Roger Dixon, Jenny Hall, Sarah Jones, Lucie Parkin, and Thomas Ward. I would also like to thank collectors around the world who have offered help and advice including: Letitia Jacopini, Masa Sunami, Tom Westerich, Stefan Wallrafen, David Nishimura, Tarek Suleimanagich, John McKenzie, Stephen Hull, and Andreas Lambrou, and also Matt Maxwell and Nick Baggott at KCJB, who although they don't know it, are latent pen collectors. My special thanks to Gerald Sattin who so kindly allowed me to photograph part of his outstanding collection, and last, but by no means least, my long-suffering and patient editor Anna Briffa.

PART I

The Story of the Fountain Pen

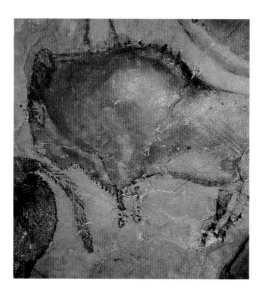

*Natural pigments were used to develop paints
for the walls of the Altamira caves, Spain,
c. 10,000 B.C.*

The Origins of the First Pen

WRITING IS ONE OF mankind's greatest skills, for it is script and writing equipment that have enabled our cultural development. It is possible that the magnificent cave paintings of the Upper Paleolithic period toward the end of the Pleistocene (the last or "Great" Ice Age) may be considered the origins of a pictorial form of writing later to find a more formal expression in Egyptian hieroglyphics. The most important surviving cave paintings are at Lascaux in the Dordogne region of France painted c.30,000–20,000 B.C., and at Altamira near Santander in northeast Spain painted by the Magdalenian peoples c.15,000–10,000 B.C. Each show spectacular polychrome animals including deer, bison, and wild boar painted in reds, blacks, yellows, and browns derived from ochers and other naturally occurring mineral pigments. The purpose and meaning of cave art remain obscure but there can be no doubt that these drawings were intended to convey a specific message to the viewer.

Primitive man was a hunter and continually on the move, with little time for language and communication beyond what was necessary for survival. With the domestication of animals and the development of farming came both the need and the time available to develop writing skills. A series of pictures linked together told a story, left a record, or recorded information for future reference. This kind of "picture writing" was further simplified into stylized images and basic strokes that were produced as easily as possible. This first writing occurred in Mesopotamia between the Tigris and Euphrates rivers where the Sumerians developed a writing system known as cuneiform. This pictographic script was reduced to angular forms to make it more suitable for impressing into wet clay tablets with a split reed, which gave the strokes a characteristic cuneiform (wedge-shaped) appearance. From the third to the first millennium B.C. the cuneiform script was adopted by successive societies in the Ancient Near East from the Sumerians to the Hittites, Babylonians, and Assyrians and came to form the basis of a number of languages as it spread through the Middle

East. Cuneiform evolved from around 2,000 writing symbols to around 600 symbols of sounds during this period, growing from a method of recording temple administration into a powerful tool for recording complex medical, astronomical, legal, and mathematical information. It was successfully deciphered between 1844 and 1857 and many remarkable texts have now been translated which authenticate Old Testament stories.

At almost the same time writing was developed in the fertile Nile valley. Here farmers recorded the annual flooding of the Nile by carving symbols on stone walls. We know this writing as "hieroglyphics" from the later Greek term for "sacred carved (letters)." The term is somewhat misleading as the script was not only used for religious inscriptions but also for monumental and secular purposes, and it was painted or written on papyrus. Unlike cuneiform, the basic structure of hieroglyphics was to remain unchanged from c.3000 B.C. to the fourth century A.D., even when the more cursive forms of hieratic and demotic script had developed from it. The writing was to remain artistic, if cumbersome, throughout its long history and was composed of three forms of symbol, each an individual picture or geometric figure; pictographs (stylized pictures), ideographs (to represent various concepts), and phonetic symbols (for 24 individual consonants).

A complete clay tablet inscribed with twenty-one lines of Sumerian cuneiform dated to the year of King Anam-sin, circa 2042 B.C. The distinctive wedge-shaped form of the characters is easily seen.

*A triple vertical panel of hieroglyphics from a black
granite statue, 26th Dynasty, circa 600 B.C.*

The Egyptians' most revolutionary contribution to writing
was the introduction of reed brush, ink, and papyrus. This
fluent and simple system arose from their search for a quicker
method of writing and is the direct ancestor of modern handwriting. Cuneiform had been simplified to increase the speed of
inscribing damp clay tablets; the new Egyptian method was so
much quicker that neither formal hieroglyphics, nor its cursive
forms—the priestly "hieratic" script and later secular "demotic"
script—needed to be abbreviated. Raw materials for writing
equipment were plentiful in Egypt. The papyrus reed (*Cyperus
papyrus*), from which the word "paper" is derived, was split
lengthways and pasted together in two layers at right angles to
each other to create an even, generous writing surface. A thin

rush plant (*Juncus maritimus*) provided writing brushes. The brush was made by crushing the end of a reed section to create natural bristles and the cell structure would absorb sufficient soot-ink for a line of writing. Despite being subject to a royal monopoly, papyrus remained a popular form of writing material in Egypt through the Greek and Roman empires and into the Middle Ages.

PARCHMENT, PAPER, AND THE QUILL PEN

The evolution of the Egyptian reed brush and papyrus into the fountain pen and paper we use today was a regular sequence of improvements to writing implements, ink, and the writing surface. Each step forward had to overcome the restrictions imposed by the physical characteristics of the materials in use at the time.

The Ancient Greeks introduced a writing instrument that was harder than the Egyptians' brush. Their reed pen was made from a harder-skinned plant, *Phragmytis communis,* and was both strong and versatile. It is possible that the new hard pen was adopted because of its similarity to the iron or wooden stylus used for notetaking on wax tablets, and was soon exported to Egypt. Papyrus continued to dominate the Mediterranean world as a writing surface until the second century B.C. By this time there was a growing demand for papyrus from the Romans in addition to the Greeks and the kingdoms of Asia Minor, leading to a shortage and a rise in prices. Pliny the Elder tells us that between 197 and 158 B.C. Ptolemy of Egypt cut off supplies of papyrus to his rival Eumenes II of Pergamon in Asia Minor in order to prevent Eumenes compiling the largest library in the world. The word "parchment" is derived from Pergamon where, it is claimed, this new smoother writing surface was developed from leather as an alternative to papyrus. Leather had in fact been used for writing from at least 2500 B.C., but it is likely Pergamon refined the process to give us the smooth, white, double-sided sheet that was to become a universal writing surface.

From the Dark Ages until the nineteenth century, the quill pen was the means by which every aspect of the growth of civilization in Europe was recorded. Almost every written work of religion, philosophy, literature, history, science, medicine, commerce, and administration relied upon the humble goose

Two quill pens showing signs of considerable re-sharpening. Feather quills were the most popular pens for nearly two thousand years, and are still used by scribes and illuminators today.

feather for its existence. However, there is considerable doubt and speculation over the date of the first quill pen. The rough surface of papyrus was not suitable for the small, fine writing which could be developed with the introduction of smooth parchment or vellum. It is possible that the Romans recognized a similarity between the hollow reed and the hollow flight-feather of a bird, but the evidence is purely circumstantial. The earliest recorded evidence of the quill pen is found in the church of San Vitale, in Ravenna, Italy. Here a mosaic, believed to have been completed before the church was dedicated on May 17, 547 A.D., shows St. Matthew writing his Gospel at a desk with both a quill and reed pen. The quill had several advantages over previous pens; it was more flexible, lasted longer, and could be cut to a finer point. It was also more widespread. It is therefore hardly surprising that it became the dominant writing implement for the best part of two millennia and no better could be found when parchment gave way to paper.

The invention of paper in China around 105 A.D. is attributed to Tsai-Lun, a eunuch and former palace guard. It was made from bamboo shoots, rags, and hemp which had been pounded, boiled, and then sieved to leave a residue which was spread into sheets and dried. Paper use and manufacture spread northwest along the trade routes and a mill was operational at Baghdad, Persia by 793 A.D. From here it spread through the Arab world, first to Damascus, then Egypt, Morocco, and finally to Xatavia in Spain where the Moors established the first paper mill in Europe by 1150. Mills were set up at Herault, France by 1189, at Fabriano, Italy in 1260, in Germany by 1389, and finally in England where a London merchant, John Tate, is recorded as making paper in 1498 during the reign of King Henry VII. Paper made from rags or plants was almost entirely superseded by wood-pulp paper during the nineteenth century.

Unlike vellum and parchment, paper was comparatively cheap and quick to produce in large quantities, essential for the development of printed books. The first printed book was the Gutenberg Bible, published in Germany in 1457 and named after Johannes Gutenberg, a goldsmith from Mainz who invented the first interchangeable typeface. Printed books accelerated the growth of literacy as professional scribes, who had formerly copied books for their living, now turned to the teaching of writing. The quills used to make pens were the five largest feathers from each wing of goose, turkey, swan, crow or duck. Feathers from other birds were sometimes used as well.

The demand for quills in England alone by the end of the nineteenth century was such that millions of geese were farmed exclusively for their feathers, supplemented by the importing of North American wild goose quills by the Hudson's Bay Company.

This superb silver quill-cutter is one of the rarest types of pocket quill-cutting machine. It has a steel key which screws down onto the quill scoop to shape and split the nib.

Preparing a quill for writing is both an art and a science. Quill pens quickly lost their sharpness in use and needed frequent recutting. A skilled scribe would be able to prolong the life of his pen by resharpening it many times with one of a variety of knives or pocket quill-cutting machines favored through the ages. It is clear that not many people were able to master this art and the majority of quills were sold ready prepared, to be discarded when blunt rather than recut.

Joseph Bramah (1749–1815), a prominent English inventor, patented a mechanical quill-cutter in 1809 which was a refinement of earlier forms. It had a significant commercial application as a quill could be cut into several strips, and each of these divided into sections from which a nib was cut. The result was several nibs cut from a single quill and sold as "Bramah's Patent Pens"—the first machine-produced nibs. These could be mounted in one of Bramah's patent holders, the quill being held in position by a swiveled grip secured by a locking ring. Many holders were made to exquisite designs in precious metals, ivory, tortoiseshell, and semiprecious stones, all eagerly sought-after by collectors today. The protection of Bramah's patent expired after 15 years and led many retailers such as Palmer, Cooper, Walsh, and Mordan to compete for business. The range and variety of quill holders grew as these firms prospered and Mordan in particular registered many unusual designs including a hand which appears to grip the nib. This increased competition caused prices for prepared quill nibs to fall from three shillings for 25 in 1809 to one shilling and sixpence per hundred in 1824, and so the quill nib remained popular until it was finally superseded by the steel pen around 1845.

Joseph Bramah's "fragment form" quill nibs of his 1809 patent and two late-Georgian holders.

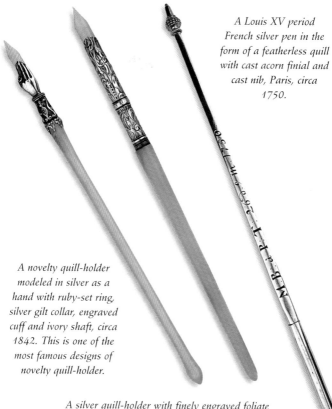

A Louis XV period French silver pen in the form of a featherless quill with cast acorn finial and cast nib, Paris, circa 1750.

A novelty quill-holder modeled in silver as a hand with ruby-set ring, silver gilt collar, engraved cuff and ivory shaft, circa 1842. This is one of the most famous designs of novelty quill-holder.

A silver quill-holder with finely engraved foliate decoration and sprung jaws secured by a sliding collar, on a mother-of-pearl shaft, circa 1840.

THE METAL PEN

The metal pen's pedigree can be traced to the metal stylus of antiquity. Numerous endeavors have been made to find a metallic substitute for the quill and thereby replace a pen which needs constant sharpening and care with one that does not. It is a common misconception that the metal pen was invented in the second half of the eighteenth century, when it was actually in use much earlier than this. A book published by John Fust and Peter Schoeiffer in 1465 refers to "ink [and] brazen reed," presumably reed-type pen fashioned from metal. In the following century a book by John Neudorffer published in 1544 refers to pens being made from "iron and copper tube, also copper and brass thin sheet."

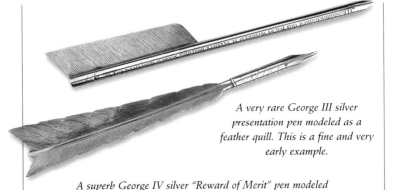

A very rare George III silver presentation pen modeled as a feather quill. This is a fine and very early example.

A superb George IV silver "Reward of Merit" pen modeled as a feather quill.

Once again technology limited the development of an idea; it was not yet possible for metal to equal the natural flexibility of a quill, and gold, which was sufficiently flexible, wore too fast. Silver pens in the form of quills survive from the 1750s onward, often with a presentation inscription and date, but they must have been heavy and cumbersome to use. There were numerous attempts to produce a metal pen throughout the sixteenth, seventeenth, and eighteenth centuries, but none were suitable for everyday writing and for mass production.

In the end it was the steel pen made from pressed sheet metal which was to become almost universal throughout the nineteenth century. Experiments had been made with the steel pen as early as the 1540s and these were produced in some quantity by the 1680s. However, it was England, at that time

Two steel pen nibs.

Two boxes of Perry & Co steel pen nibs. The steel pen nib became almost universal during the nineteenth century and Britain led the world in their production.

the leading industrial nation in Europe, who produced the first cheap, mass-produced, reliable steel pen nibs. Samuel Harrison of Birmingham is the first recorded maker, around 1780, and John Mitchell, also of Birmingham, the man who made a breakthrough with machine production. In 1830 James Perry improved the elasticity of the steel pen by making short slits on the shoulder, parallel to the main one. The following year yet another Birmingham manufacturer, Joseph Gillot, made the final refinements and produced a metal pen that could finally compete on equal terms with the quill. Annual production of Gillot nibs in the eight years from 1842 to 1850 rose from 70 million to a staggering 180 million.

While the importance of the steel pen cannot be underestimated in the history of writing equipment, it was the continued development of the gold pen in the 1820s which was to play an important and direct role in the history of the fountain pen. By about 1822 William Doughty, a London watchmaker, had started manufacturing and selling pens with a v-shaped gold nib tipped with rubies and cut and set by a local lapidary John Rose. It is possible that Rose, not Doughty, had invented the process, which would explain why Doughty did not patent the design. Doughty's "ruby-pointed pens" were expensive and the holders usually made from luxury materials such as tortoiseshell set with gold piqué. Doughty pointed out that they were economical, however, because they lasted for several years, and soon other makers were producing them too.

The British scientist William Hyde Woolaston had discovered the production of malleable platinum just after 1800, and research eventually led to the discovery of four metallic elements—iridium, osmium, palladium, and rhodium. Woolaston produced an extremely hard rhodium-tin alloy which was suitable for pen tips. This discovery occurred around 1822 and by 1825 Woolaston estimated that he had produced enough alloy for around 6,500 pens. The alloy was sold to T. C. Robinson, a London instrument maker and manufacturer of ruby-pointed pens, who fused the iridium tips to flexible gold nibs. Osmium-iridium, another of Woolaston's alloys, was rejected by Robinson as too hard to grind for pen manufacture, and was later taken up by John Isaac Hawkins. Between 1833 and 1834 Hawkins made a special lathe capable of giving 10,000 revolutions per minute, enabling him to make an iridium-tipped

Unusual silver extending Doughty pen with reeded body and hobnail seal terminal, nib stamped DOUGHTY circa 1825.

An important documentary 18ct. Doughty pen circa 1825, nib stamped ROSE INVENIT & JEWEL.ᴿ DOUGHTY FECIT. This pen is important evidence that Rose, not Doughty, invented the ruby-pointed pen, and therefore explains why Doughty did not patent it himself.

Side view of an 18ct. gold Doughty pen inset with gold piqué leaves and mother-of-pearl flower heads. Nib stamped DOUGHTY FECIT, circa 1825.

pen. A shortage of iridium led Hawkins to sell the business in August 1835 to Simeon Hyde of New York. The making of iridium-pointed pens was a great success in America and the number of manufacturers increased rapidly. The widespread availability of these nibs was soon to play a vital role in the birth and development of the first truly efficient fountain pens.

A large Aiken & Co. gold pen nib made in New York during the late nineteenth century. It was the widespread availability of this type of nib which played a vital role in the development of the fountain pen.

Early Reservoir Pens

EARLY ATTEMPTS AT A RESERVOIR PEN

Many attempts have been made through the ages to provide the pen with its own continuous ink supply. The earliest mention of a successful pen is that made for Caliph Mu'izz who established the Fatmid dynasty in Egypt in 969 A.D. His perfectly working gold pen is described in a manuscript book written between 969 and 975 A.D. called *Kitab al-Majalis wa'l Musa'irat* (Book of Assemblies and Discussions), a copy of which is in the library of the School of Oriental and African Studies of the University of London. The significance of this reference to the fountain pen was first appreciated by the scholar Hassan El-Basha Mamoud who translated and published the passage in 1951.

A simple form of quill pen supplied with a reservoir is described and illustrated by Daniel Schwenter in his *Deliciae Physic-Mathematicae* published in Nuremberg in 1636 and a later edition published in Zurich in 1651. This pen was composed of an inner and an outer quill. The inner quill had a small hole at the rounded end which was filled with ink and the open end then sealed. This was inserted into a quill prepared with a nib, the hole in the inner quill in alignment with the cut nib of the outer. The ink supply was released by squeezing the pen. These pens have not survived, but the idea of a "pen within a pen" lived on and was used as recently as the early years of this century by De La Rue with their Pelican pen.

The simple concept of a quill reservoir within a quill pen illustrated in Daniel Schwenter's "Deliciae Physic-Mathematicae" published in 1636.

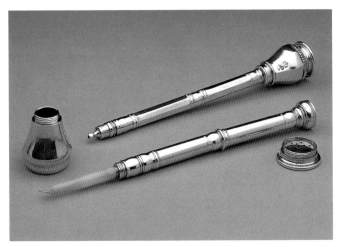

A George II silver penner of the finest quality. This is the final form of the pen probably referred to by Samuel Pepys in his Diary.

THE PENNER

The earliest and best-known reference to what is believed to be a fountain pen in English is made by Samuel Pepys in his *Diary* for August 5, 1663: "This evening came a letter about business from Mr. Coventry, and with it a silver pen he promised me to carry ink in, which is very necessary."

Pepys commented favorably on the ability to carry a pen containing ink about with him on his travels in his *Diary* on other occasions, and as he gave no detailed description of it, there has been much speculation about its appearance. It is likely that Pepys was referring to a Penner rather than a fountain pen. A full discussion of the Penner is beyond the scope of this book, but it should nevertheless be mentioned as an important and enduring stage in the history of writing instruments. Known since the Middle Ages, the Penner was to reach its most refined form at the end of the seventeenth century (when Pepys was writing) and the early eighteenth century. It was a pen with its own ink supply, albeit in a reservoir screwed onto the end, and often carried a pencil with wafers and/or a sander. The Penner must be regarded as fulfilling at least some of the essential requirements of a reservoir or fountain pen but has often been ignored or misunderstood by collectors.

A Louis XIV silver writing etui of superb quality. A writing etui such as this would have been one of the most luxurious available during Samuel Pepys's lifetime.

MONSIEUR BION'S "PLUME SANS FIN"

Nicholas Bion (d.1715), chief instrument maker to King Louis XIV of France, published a drawing and description of a "plume sans fin" (literally a never-ending pen) in his *Construction and Principle of Mathematical Instruments,* which was translated into English in 1723. This pen was to be used for nearly a century. The earliest surviving pen based on the Bion principle is dated 1702. A drawing of a similar pen was published in 1764, and Bion-pattern pens are known to have been made as late as the 1770s. The eighteenth century was the great age of instrument making and the longevity of Bion's pen is probably an indication of its success rather than a reflection of the slow progress in fountain pen improvement.

The Bion-pattern pen worked on a simple principle. The hollow pen body acted as a reservoir and was sealed at one end by a cork or stopper. A prepared quill pen was screwed around a slim pipe at the other end and the pen was sealed by a cap. The cap fitted over the nib, and a slender plug prevented the ink from leaking through the pipe. On some later examples the quill had

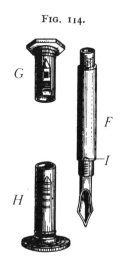

Fig. 114.

Engraving of Bion's pen.

*A George II silver fountain pen of exceptional quality
with its original rayskin case circa 1750.*

been superseded by a metal nib. In order to use the pen, the cap
was removed and the pen shaken every time ink needed to be
transferred from the reservoir, through the pipe, to the nib. The
Bion pen was normally made of brass, but leading makers in
London or Paris also supplied orders in gold and silver,
sometimes covered with fashionable material such as mother-
of-pearl.

FÖLSCH'S AND BRAMAH'S PATENTS (1809)

Numerous patents for reservoir pens were granted throughout
the nineteenth century from the early reservoir pens which
merely contained an ink supply to the later fountain pens where
the ink also flowed in a regular and controlled manner.

The first English patent was granted to Frederick Fölsch of
Oxford Street, London in May 1809. His pen is recognized by its
spring-loaded plunger used to increase the flow of ink from the
barrel to the nib. This pen is important because it was the first
to do more than just deliver a supply of ink to its nib. Fölsch
recognized that the ink chamber needed to be kept at an even
pressure and that air needed to come through to the reservoir to
replace the ink that had flowed out. Two of his improvements
achieved this. The first, a hole cut in the bottom of the cylindrical metal nib above the ink feed was able "to admit the air,
and adjust the quantity of ink it will bear"; the second was a
groove in the nib, "to guide the ink to a point."

Joseph Bramah's patent of September 1809 was mainly con-
cerned with quill-cutting but it also made an important
contribution to the development of the fountain pen. He
invented what was to become the fountain pen "feed"—that
vital piece which conveys ink under the nib from the reservoir

An important Louis XV period fountain pen made on the Bion principle, crafted throughout in 18ct. gold and brass and faced with panels of mother-of-pearl. Paris hallmark for 1768–1774.

to the pen point. His feed was a piece of cork with "a small groove, not larger in dimensions than the smallest pinhole" designed to carry ink by capillary action. It is unlikely to have been entirely reliable as the inks of the time were prone to clogging with small particles. No example of the Bramah pen has been found by collectors.

Recognition of these improvements to air-flow and the ink feed were to be the basis of the future development of the fountain pen.

JOHN SCHEFFER'S PATENT (1819)

John Scheffer's patent, granted in 1819, was not a radical step forward but his design was a commercial success and, as it was used well into the 1840s, the pen must have been fairly reliable. An early advertisement claimed that Scheffer's pen would write for 10–12 hours without having to be refilled. The Penographic or Writing Instrument, as it was known, returned to the two-tube system; an

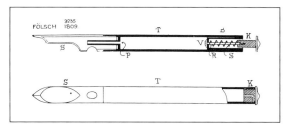

A diagram of Fölsch's pen, clearly showing the hole in the bottom of the nib to admit air to the reservoir and equalize the pressure. There are no known surviving examples of this pen at present.

inner reservoir made of quill and sheep gut, and an outer case of silver or gold. The pen could be fitted with either a quill or metal nib. A button on the side of the pen squeezed ink from the internal container, and there was a small lever-operated ink-cock (a shut-off valve) which could seal the pen when not in use and prevent the ink from drying out. As a safety measure, and in order to prevent unwanted accidents, the cap could only be placed on the pen when the cock was retracted to the closed position.

An original Penographic is rare to find and eagerly sought after by collectors. They are sometimes difficult to identify as they do not bear the Scheffer mark and the patent or license to manufacture it seems to have changed hands several times. The earliest examples were sold by W. Robson & Co. of St. Dunstan's Hill, London. These are marked "W. ROBSON & CO. PATENTEES LONDON" and for the first two or three years appear to have been made for Robson by John Cottrill of Birmingham. However, this can not be proven from 1822 on, since they bear the silver hallmark of William Robson. The design was improved around 1824–25, presumably by Robson, and the use of the ink-cock was discontinued. In 1826–27 both Robson and J. H. Farthing were advertising almost identical Penographs; but by the 1840s manufacture seems to have passed to Mordan & Co. who advertised it as a "self-supplying pen."

A silver Scheffer's Patented "Penographic" fountain pen made under license by W. Robson & Co., with additional feature of a sliding pencil.

JOHN JACOB PARKER'S
PATENT (1832)

Parker's pen was an important and fundamental move forward; not only did it acknowledge the importance of atmospheric equalization, but it was also the first fountain pen to be self-filling. The reservoir was lined with glass or gold to counteract ink corrosion and was filled with a piston mechanism, unlike previous pens which had required ink to be poured into the reservoir through a funnel. Parker's pen was filled by dipping the penholder into ink and raising the piston by turning the outer case; ink was thus drawn into the resulting vacuum. The piston could be lowered to deliver ink through a small bell-mouthed tube to the quill nib. The pen was sealed by a wire attached to the inside of the cap which entered the ink-delivering passage and closed it, preventing leakage.

Both Parker and Scheffer pens were numbered sequentially as they were made, and it is therefore possible to compare their development. Scheffer Penographic No. 3396 was hallmarked in 1825, indicating that sales averaged around 500 per annum during the first seven years of production. Parker No. 6047 was hallmarked in 1833, only the second year of production. From this it would seem that this new self-filling pen found immediate and widespread acceptance, selling nearly 12 times faster than the earlier pen.

A silver John Jacob Parker's Patented "Self-Filling" fountain pen, 1832.

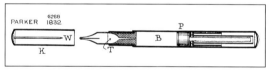

Cross-section of Parker's Pen.

GOODYEAR'S PATENT (1851) AND OTHER DEVELOPMENTS

It was a manufacturing process, rather than a pen, which was to be the next step toward a viable fountain pen. Goodyear patented a process for the treatment of latex rubber with sulfur to create a hardened material known variously as vulcanite, ebonite, or hard rubber. Rods in hard rubber could be worked with a drill or turned on a lathe and, compared to gold or silver, it was easy and cheap to make in quantity. Hard rubber was to become the favored material for fountain pens until it was replaced by plastic in the late 1920s. Prince's patent of 1855 and Moseley's of 1859 used the new hard rubber for their pens.

Throughout the next two decades there was little radical change in the design of the fountain pen although advances were made in other fields. In the 1860s ink became finer and its texture more consistent, free of the particles that would clog a pen. Steel nibs were corroded by this new chemical ink, however, and so production increased of iridium-tipped gold nibs which did not corrode when used with the ink.

By the end of the 1870s all the requirements for the so-called modern fountain pen production had been met—except one: Hard rubber for pen parts was inexpensive and freely available in quantity, ink was consistent and free-flowing, and hard-wearing gold nibs were being mass produced. Numerous fountain pens were on the market, yet none had fulfilled the ultimate requirement—a reliable, regular ink flow. This became the achievement of the early 1880s and ensured lasting supremacy for the fountain pen over the quill and steel pens.

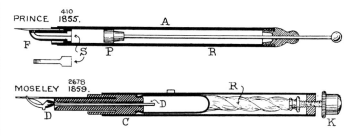

Both Prince's patent of 1855 and Moseley's of 1859 used the new hard rubber for their pens; however there was little improvement on either the piston or the bladder patented by Parker and Scheffer.

Fountain Pens from 1880 to Present

THE BIRTH OF THE MODERN FOUNTAIN PEN

It is a common misconception that L.E. Waterman invented the fountain pen in 1884, largely owing to an elaborate story told originally by Waterman himself. He is famous as the first American sufficiently astute to patent a channeled feed but he was not the first person to invent it. As we have seen, Joseph Bramah's 1809 pen employed a channeled feed, and other pioneers of the reservoir pen including Fölsch and J.J. Parker also appreciated the importance of atmospheric equalization. It is conceivable that the modern fountain pen would have been produced 60 or 70 years earlier had these pioneers enjoyed the benefits of the free-flowing inks, gold nibs, and inexpensive hard-rubber holders available to Waterman in the 1880s.

Lewis Edson Waterman was an insurance salesman in New York, not an inventor. Legend has it that he lost an important sale when his pen leaked ink over the contract and by the time he had another drawn up a rival had stolen his business; Waterman resolved to use a reliable pen—even if he had to make it himself.

On February 12, 1884 Waterman was granted his first patent. His pen enabled ink to flow from the reservoir to the nib by capillary action along a channel in the feed, while an equal volume of air entered the reservoir through fine cuts sawn in the base of this same channel.

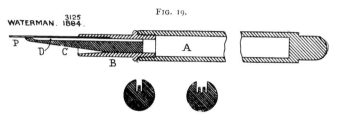

Cross-section of a pen using Waterman's 1884 patent.

1880–1920

An extraordinary creativity characterizes the early years of commercial fountain-pen production. In the 1880s numerous pens were designed quite independently of each other which, like Waterman's, were improvements on the existing pens of the day. Once the reliable feed became widespread, attention focussed once again on producing a clean and preferably self-filling pen.

The first pens were filled by dropping ink into them with a pipette (or "eye-dropper"). This system was to remain popular until World War I and in some tropical countries remained in use even longer. It was a somewhat messy process, however, and so the self-filling pen was developed using one of two familiar designs, the piston dating back to J.J. Parker, and the ink-sac expounded by Scheffer. Although the piston was employed by many manufacturers, it did not come to be considered reliable until improvements were made to it in the late 1920s. The notable exception is De La Rue's Onoto pen, whose plunger system filled on the downstroke and was used from 1905 to the 1940s, achieving great success throughout the world.

The ink-sac was used more widely after 1900. At first there was a diverse range of filling systems employed to fill the flexible rubber sac through a solid pen barrel, including Roy Conklin's Crescent Filler of 1901. Here a pressure bar ran along the length of the sac to compress it and, when released, the sac expanded and drew ink into the pen. The bar was operated by a metal crescent protruding through the barrel and when not in use for filling was held in place with a locking ring. Soon the pressure bar was to be operated by less obtrusive means, the side lever patented by Walter A. Sheaffer on August 25, 1908, and the end-button-filler patented by George S. Parker in 1904. However, Parker was slow to see the demand for self-filling

FIG. 101.

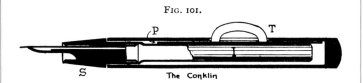

Cross-section of Roy Conklin's pen.

W. A. Sheaffer's lever-filling system.

pens and delayed production of the button-filler until he felt the competition from Sheaffer who had taken out a second patent on December 10, 1912. The lever and the button were to remain the industry standard until well after World War II.

It is a myth that, like the Model-T Ford, all pens at this time were black. The majority were black hard rubber, and only a minority made of red or mottled hard rubber (a combination of the two), but pens were often engraved with delicate designs and adorned with decorative metal mounts. Jewelers were employed by the leading manufacturers to enrich their pens with luxurious gold, silver, and filigree overlays in a wide variety of designs, often incorporating mother-of-pearl, semiprecious stones, and jewels. These pens are eagerly sought-after today and some, like the Parker "Snake" pen, have become legendary among collectors.

THE 1920S AND 1930S

The 1920s are usually regarded as the golden age of the fountain pen. Mass-market pens, which with the advent of plastics had become a riot of color, came to be a fashion statement. Design flair and effective marketing were as important in maintaining the market share as each technical advance.

Parker entered the twenties with a new top-of-the-range pen called the Duofold. It became an instant classic and has influenced manufacturers and designers to this day. It employed the design improvements George Parker had made since the turn of the

century, the most important of which were mechanical filling (1904), improved "spear" feeds (1905 and 1911), the screw-on cap (1912), and the washer pocket-clip (1916). These features were part of the existing Jack-knife range, but combined with the colored pen with which George Parker had first experimented in 1904, the result was spectacular. The new pen was larger, more colorful, and—at $7—more than twice the price of the average pen. George's son, Kenneth Parker, masterminded the sales and advertising campaign which launched the pen in 1921, and watched one week's sales match the cost of the intensive three-month promotion.

Three years later, in 1924, Sheaffer took an important step forward in pen design with the launch of a pen of unbreakable plastic. Pens were now stronger than the brittle hard rubber examples and for the first time could be made in a range of colors. This plastic was made from cellulose nitrate and called celluloid by Dupont, its main manufacturer. It was quickly adopted by many pen companies who called it by a variety of names: Sheaffer used "Radite," Parker "Permanite," Wahl-Eversharp "Pyralin," and so on. The first plastic pens were made in plain colors, but by 1928 marbled plastics were in use, and after this new colors, combinations, and styles quickly came to be produced.

During the Depression, following the Wall Street crash of 1929, Parker developed a new

The original Parker Lucky-Curve Duofold introduced in 1921 was big, bold, and bright and still influences pen design to this day.

A selection of Sheaffer pens made from the late 1920s to early 1940s and showing the variety of celluloid products used. Dupont's product code can be seen clearly on two pens (center bottom).

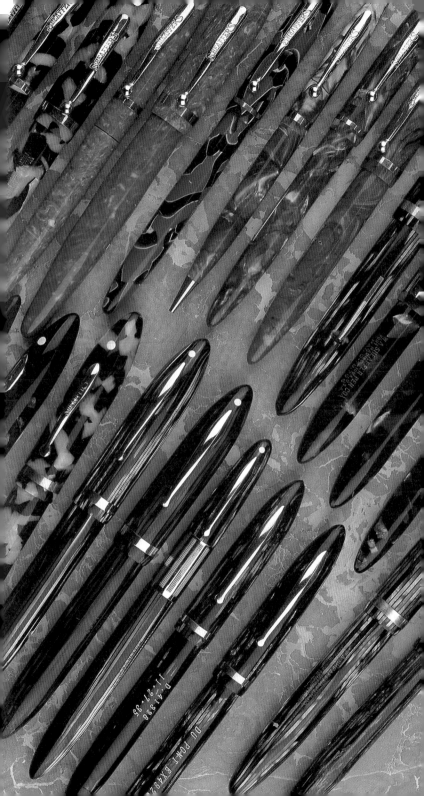

filling mechanism. A radical new pen was launched, the Vacumatic, which was advertised as holding 102% more ink than previous pens and an ink supply visible through windows in the unique laminated plastic barrel. This was only the first of many laminated plastic pens with a visible ink supply; before long Sheaffer, Waterman, Conklin, Wahl-Eversharp, and other manufacturers had all launched similar products. The visible ink supply was a short-lived fad, however, as dried ink soon made the windows difficult to see through, and many of the ingenious filling systems developed during the thirties were abandoned during World War II.

In Europe two other mechanisms were being developed. Jif-Waterman, the semiautonomous French arm of L.E. Waterman, introduced the cartridge pen in 1927. It used a glass cartridge and was an improvement on the similar Eagle fountain pen of the 1890s, but was used only for the French market and the system was not widely adopted until the 1960s.

The other lasting filling system developed in Europe at this time was the piston filler, familiar to anybody who has ever used a Montblanc today. It was developed for the German stationery manufacturers Pelikan between 1925 and 1929 by Theodor Kovács and Caroly Bako and used a piston with differential threading which cleaned the transparent ink-reservoir every time the pen was filled. When the pen was launched the mechanical parts were made with typical German precision and soon became one of the best-selling writing instruments; Montblanc retaliated with their telescopic piston filler, launched in 1935.

The Parker Vacumatic started a craze for pens with a visible ink supply and was widely imitated throughout the world.

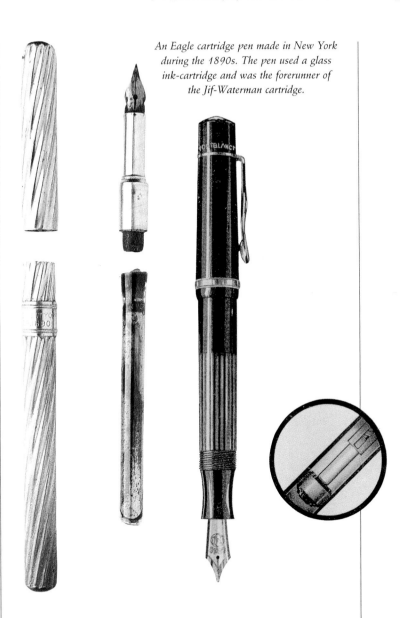

An Eagle cartridge pen made in New York during the 1890s. The pen used a glass ink-cartridge and was the forerunner of the Jif-Waterman cartridge.

This advertisement shows the modern piston-filling system which was developed in Europe between the World Wars. Here a telescopic mechanism offers an increased ink capacity as the whole of the barrel is used as a reservoir.

THE 1940S THROUGH THE 1960S

World War II brought mixed fortunes to the writing-implement industry. Many companies reverted to sac-filling pens, designs became austere, the range of pens reduced, and quality sometimes fell. The first successful ballpoint pen—the Biro—was launched in 1944 and its phenomenal success caused several smaller pen manufacturers to become extinct.

It was not all bad news, however. The Parker 51 pen was launched in 1941 and has become the world's best-selling pen, clocking up sales in excess of 41,000,000 units between 1941 and 1972, totaling around $400 million. It used the new Parker quick-drying ink (Quink), had a new smooth-writing tubular nib, and always wrote first time. It was the first totally reliable modern fountain pen, and its slender shape, slim metal cap, and hooded nib influenced pen designers around the world for many years.

After a century and a half of experimentation the ink cartridge was finally perfected with the

The legendary Parker 51 pen, regarded by many as the best pen ever made.

Field Marshal Montgomery using a Parker 51 to sign the treaty of Germany's surrender, Berlin, June 6, 1945.

aid of modern injection-technology. In 1953 Jif-Waterman launched the C.F. (Cartridge-Filler), which was to become one of their best-sellers, despite competition from Sheaffer who launched their cartridge pen in 1955, and other companies who quickly followed suit. The name of Parker's first cartridge pen, the 45, captured the convenience of the new system and was advertised as being as easy to load as the Colt .45 revolver. Cartridges were clean, convenient, and could be carried in your pocket, unlike a bottle of ink.

THE 1970S

The seventies pen was formed in the image of a fashionable design ideal, rather than to meet the needs of the writer. Pens were given an exaggerated slim-line shape and were made from stainless steel or similar materials strong enough to make small diameters and thin walls. Some of these pens are hailed as design classics by those who believed that form and function were one and the same; the Aurora Hastil was even given a place within the hallowed portals of MOMA, the Museum of Modern Art in New York.

In 1970 Parker launched a futuristic pen made almost entirely of titanium called the T-1. This pen had a space age look with its rocket-like styling and sleek integral nib unit. The pen utilized a small screw which could adjust the nib width to reflect the writer's desired writing style. Titanium is one of the toughest metals known to man, and the T-1 was soon discontinued, reputedly because of the technical problems encountered in using 1970s machinery to work a twenty-first century material. The pen was succeeded by the Parker Falcon now best-known as the first pen since the quill without a separate nib.

The titanium Parker T-1, made for just one year in 1970. Thirty years after it was designed it still looks like a pen from the future.

MODERN FOUNTAIN PENS

Today's pen manufacturers are free to plunder the best designs from the past, and are able to combine them with the finest modern technology. Many state-of-the-art pens now have a period feel about them, and while companies look back on their past glories, it seems that the fountain pen is entering another golden age. Sales are healthier than they have been for decades and the quality, range, and availability of fountain pens and matching accessories is greater than ever before.

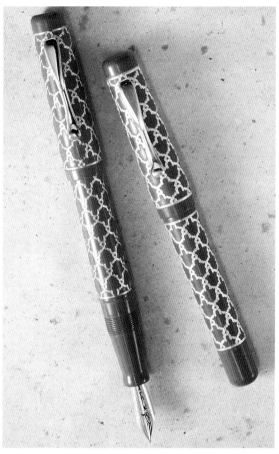

The Visconti Alhambra epitomizes the modern luxury fountain pen. It has a strong sense of tradition and quality and is made with innovative modern technology and design.

Choosing the Right Fountain Pen

WE ARE OFTEN TOLD that a pen is better for our handwriting—but why should this be so? There are several reasons why a fountain pen is superior to the convenience of a ballpoint, rollerball, or fiber-tip pen.

A fountain pen is an expressive instrument. The width of the line it makes on the paper depends on the pressure applied to the nib. A good fountain pen will reflect every change in pressure from the finest line to the broadest. These changes of pressure are what gives each person's handwriting its unique character and cannot be expressed by a ballpoint or other writing implement with a point of uniform width.

Secondly, the angle at which a ballpoint or rollerball writes best is not a natural handwriting position. In order to achieve steady control and even writing these pens need to be held closer to the vertical and at a much steeper angle than that comfortable for handwriting. This leads to cramped and tired hands and does not encourage individual handwriting. For this reason the ballpoint pen is banned in the schools of many European countries, and frowned upon in several others.

More than 20 different nib grades and styles are available for today's leading fountain pens, and the right one can be selected to suit your individual handwriting style. This is a huge advantage over ballpoints and fiber-tips, many of which don't even offer the choice of fine, medium, or broad points. The main types of nib are the following:

STANDARD These are the familiar range of fine, medium, and broad. Many companies offer a wider selection which often range from needlepoint (extra-extra fine) to spade (triple broad). These are usually available at most specialist shops (see pp.190–191) or by special order elsewhere. As a general rule, a fine nib is suitable for those with a light hand or small writing; a broader nib for bolder writing or writers who exert greater pressure. The nib you choose will largely be a matter of personal preference. It should be pointed out that a needlepoint nib is intended for precise figure work, and is not suitable for general writing.

ITALIC An italic nib has a sharp, chiseled edge (rather than the rounded ball of a standard nib) giving a thick line on the downstroke and a thin line on the cross-stroke. Italic nibs are available in a variety of widths—the broader the nib, the greater the contrast between the broad and fine strokes. The chiseled edge of the italic nib grips the paper and the writer takes more care in forming his characters. An italic nib should be slanted at 45 degrees to the page to prevent the script taking on a square and boxy appearance. The widest italic nibs are calligraphic nibs.

OBLIQUE An oblique nib is cut at an angle of 15 degrees left. It is suited to the many people who hold their pen at an angle, which puts greater pressure on one side of the nib and can cause an irregular ink flow. Oblique nibs are available from fine through to extra and triple broad and often give both a thick and thin effect but not as exaggerated as an italic nib.

REVERSE-OBLIQUE The mirror image of an oblique nib, generally used by left-handed writers.

OBLIQUE ITALIC This nib is suited to those who wish to adopt the general principles of italic writing but without too painstaking an approach. It provides a more casual way of following the italic style and gives handwriting an improved appearance. There are often two versions of oblique italic nib, 15 degrees for right-handed writers and 30 degrees, suitable for left-handed writers.

STUB Produced by several companies today, a stub nib is a broad nib that is neither rounded nor a chiseled italic. It produces thick and thin lines with a quicker hand than an italic nib, but provides less contrast.

FLEXIBILITY The flexibility of a nib varies from company to company, and each will have its own characteristics. The points of a flexible nib will part during the downstroke with a little pressure giving a traditional copperplate effect. Some companies no longer make flexible nibs as too many are damaged by heavy-fisted writers, used to a ballpoint, who then return it for a refund! This trend is starting to be reversed as we relearn the traditional art of writing.

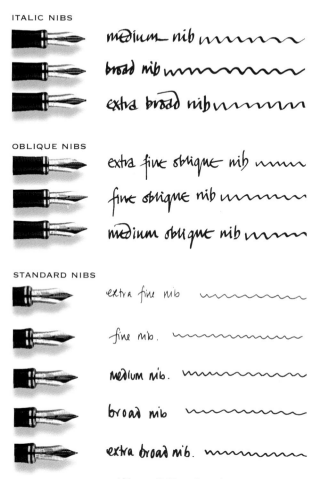

ITALIC NIBS

medium nib

broad nib

extra broad nib

OBLIQUE NIBS

extra fine oblique nib

fine oblique nib

medium oblique nib

STANDARD NIBS

extra fine nib

fine nib.

medium nib.

broad nib

extra broad nib.

*Nibs available with Parker's
Duofold Centennial pen.*

The majority of quality fountain pen nibs today are made of gold, usually 14ct., but sometimes 18ct., to create a luxurious feel. As gold is a soft, flexible metal, a gold nib is usually tipped with a ball of extremely hard metal alloy such as iridium or ruthenium, which is ground and polished to a perfect writing surface. A nib can be firm or flexible depending on the thickness of the gold and the length of the point, and will vary from company to company. It is always worth testing several brands of pen as well as nib types to find the style that suits you best.

Cheaper pens tend to have steel or gold-plated metal nibs. Unlike gold nibs, they are unlikely to last a lifetime but they are certainly not to be dismissed as inferior. The general maxim is that a gold nib will wear in and a steel nib wear out, but quality varies between manufacturers and you may well be lucky enough to buy a pen with a steel nib that will last for years.

When choosing a fountain pen you should not just select something that looks nice or is fashionable; when someone receives a letter or document that you have written they will see your writing and not the pen you used. The right pen will feel comfortable in your hand and will write effortlessly. Choose the correct type of pen and the best nib to suit your style of writing. Pens are made in different sizes and weights for a good reason; if you have small hands or tire when using a heavy pen, don't be afraid to opt for something which isn't the biggest pen in the shop or the one covered in the most gold. Finally, when trying out a pen remember to sit at a desk or table; many people forget this and try out a pen stooped over a shop counter in an unfamiliar writing position and then find that the pen feels uncomfortable when they use it at home or in their office.

An advertisement from Parker, 1944, telling the customer exactly why the new 51 is the right pen to buy.

Ink: The Pen's Companion

INK IS VERY MUCH the pen's companion; just as the pen has evolved through the ages, so has the ink used with it.

In the Ancient World ink-cakes were used that were made from soot or lamp black mixed with gum in much the same way as Chinese stick-ink is used today. When a saucer of ink was required the block was rubbed down with a little water, giving a dense, lasting black ink with little tendency to fade through the millennia. Our word for ink derives from the Latin *encaustum*, thought to be a more caustic form of ink used by the Romans and made with a mild acid, such as vinegar, which would have bitten into the surface of papyrus or parchment giving greater permanence to the writing. Red ink was made from vermilion and both were treated almost as paint by scribes using the square-cut reed brush, or split-reed pen in use at that time.

A more free-flowing ink was favored for use with the quill pen from the early medieval period to the nineteenth century. This iron-gall ink was made from tannins extracted from a range of vegetable sources and often traded from as far afield as the Levant or Barbary coast. Ink manufacture was widespread and numerous recipes survive from the Middle Ages giving formulas and methods of ink manufacture. In a fairly lengthy process lasting some weeks the tannins were converted to gallic acid and then combined with ferrous sulfate, resulting in a wonderful blue-black ink.

Vintage bottles of Parker Quink, the first ink developed for use with a specific fountain pen.

These two traditional inks did not suit the mass-produced steel pen developed in the second quarter of the nineteenth century. Carbon ink tended to clog and was difficult to store in bottles, while the acid iron-gall ink corroded the point of steel pens. Chemical ink dyes seemed to offer a solution; Henry Stephens was granted a patent in 1834 and James Perry developed his ink in the early 1840s. The discovery of aniline dyes in 1856 revolutionized ink manufacture, enabling the production of a range of colored inks which were free-flowing but did not spread into the paper.

The range of ink available by the 1920s would bewilder many people today. It is estimated that the German firm Pelikan alone produced 172 different types, colors, or bottles of ink. There were inks for writing, for drawing, for accountants (which could not be erased), for hoteliers (which could be erased) and so on. Many of these special inks are still available now, each with a different consistency and its own special properties. Fountain-pen ink is designed specifically for use in fountain pens; if you are considering using a drawing, lettering, or technical pen it is important to use the appropriate ink.

Fountain pen companies marketed proprietary brands of ink in the 1920s but it is likely that there was little difference between them at this time. Reading between the lines of a Waterman's sales manual of 1926 one senses that it was not so much the ink that was important as the packaging—a screw-top bottle which had no need for a crumbling stopper and excluded dust, both of which would clog a fountain pen. Parker, Mabie Todd, De La Rue, and Montblanc all marketed special ink containers at this time which are eagerly sought-after today.

The first ink developed specifically for use with a particular fountain pen was Parker Quink, launched in 1933. So-called because it was quick-drying, it contained a secret ingredient, "Solv-X," a special solvent designed to clean the materials used to make Parker components. Over the years other companies have followed suit, developing and marketing inks to enhance the performance of their pens. While most of these inks are suitable for a wide range of pens, the chemical composition of some brands has an adverse reaction with the mechanism of other brands of pen. If in doubt it is best to follow what the manufacturer recommends for each brand rather than have a leaking or clogged pen.

PART II

The Fountain Pen Directory

SHEAFFER'S
PEN — PENCIL

"I call it my true Companion."

YES, the SHEAFFER Fountain Pen, though a small, is a faithful companion, it says to those light hearts who receive it at graduation or on any other gift occasion: "The one who sent me was not only generous in his gift, but thoughtful in his concern for your happiness. Generous because he paid the price of the most beautiful of gifts, thoughtful because he was constant in obtaining the SHEAFFER which will never fizzle over Uncle's fingers with its stains, but cause the shadow of a frown to cross your brow through failure to write at your bidding." Ask at leading stations or write for catalog.

Illustrated—Fits No. 04, short ebony finish with gold-filled band, $8.75

W. A. SHEAFFER PEN COMPANY, 220 SHEAFFER BUILDING, FORT MADISON, IOWA

NEW YORK · CHICAGO · KANSAS CITY · SAN FRANCISCO

SHEAFFER-1920

Key to Directory Section

THE SELECTED LIST of manufacturers and fountain pens in this section does not claim to be totally comprehensive, but it should contain most of the brands you are likely to come across, as well as some lesser-known makes that cannot be overlooked.

The Company Facts box, offers immediate information including the location of the company, its factory and distribution. The following key provides an explanation of the symbols used.

Each company varies enormously in the kind of products they sell. In some cases, for example Cartier, the fountain pens are just one product among a large variety of luxury goods, such as wristwatches, lighters, and leather accessories. In other cases, for example Hakase, the handmade fountain pen is the only product made by the company, although available in several finishes. In addition to this some companies design limited-edition casings for pens made by well-known brands such as Sheaffer and Aurora.

As a result of this large variety, and in order to make the information given as comprehensible as possible, *The Company Products* box lists just the current line(s) of fountain pens available. In some cases this will be a single name, and in others it will be a full list of up to eight lines made. Other products, such as leather goods, watches, pencils, technical pens etc, are not listed in full. Many of the companies featured produce limited editions, and those of greater interest have been selected in each case, but not listed individually in the product box, since they change with some frequency.

COMPANY FACTS

EST. Date when company was established

Location of headquarters

Location of factory

Lists where products are distributed

$ Star-rating system to give an idea of price:

★ under $100
★★ low hundreds
★★★ high hundreds
★★★★ thousands

Alfred Dunhill

T HE DUNHILL-NAMIKI COLLABORATION (see pp.48–54) is by
no means the sole extent of Alfred Dunhill's ventures into
the world of fountain pens. This well-known English company's
writing instruments have enjoyed popularity both before and
after the 1930s Dunhill-Namiki.

Alfred Dunhill.

Since starting his business in 1893,
Alfred Dunhill demonstrated a
rare creative talent in designing a
wide range of innovative products
of superlative quality. He is well-
known as the inventor of the
modern pocket cigarette lighter,
but less well-known is his
contribution to the development
of the "drop-action" pencil and
the 1930s watch pen. It would be
possible to fill several books with
the achievements of this
quintessentially English family
firm which has grown to serve the worldwide needs of the
international luxury market.

During the 1960s and 1970s Alfred Dunhill's collection of
writing instruments included the Broadstroke and the Generation
I, sometimes produced in 18-ct. gold or platinum encrusted with
diamonds. Dunhill was expanding into men's fashion,
fragrances, and accessories and was looking for a quality
manufacturer for its writing instruments. In 1977 it acquired a
majority shareholding in Montblanc, the famous German
marque (see pp.118–125), taking over the company in 1985.

COMPANY PRODUCTS

Known for luxury gentlemen's goods and accessories

DRESS PEN
GEMLINE

NIBS: four

Alfred Dunhill has been part of the Vendôme Luxury Group since October 1993, an umbrella company which combines Cartier, Alfred Dunhill, Montblanc, Piaget, Baume & Mercier, Karl Lagerfeld, Chloe, Sulka, Hackett, and Seeger. The company is still managed as a family concern with Richard Dunhill at the reins and his son Mark Dunhill overseeing the writing-instrument division.

COMPANY FACTS	
EST.	1893
	London, England
	Branches worldwide
$	★ ★

Examples of both a watch and lighters currently available from Alfred Dunhill's line of luxury goods. Of superlative quality, they appeal to a clientele of discerning taste.

DRESS PEN

GEMLINE

DRESS PEN

The Dress Pen is derived from the Dunhill watch pen of the 1930s and shares the same flat profile. The collection is available in fountain pen, ballpoint, pencil, and convertible rollerball/ballpoint. The finishes are either gold- or silver-plate with matching trim, or alternatively with black, blue or green lacquer detailing. Each pen has a sprung clip and individual serial number. They are very much part of the cosmopolitan style now favored by Dunhill.

GEMLINE

The Gemline is a traditional cylindrical pen and ballpoint available in silver-plate, gold-plate, and black lacquer, in keeping with Dunhill's modern image.

Alfred Dunhill-Namiki

TODAY DUNHILL-NAMIKI PENS RECEIVE universal acclaim as the most luxurious vintage fountain pens, sought-after by many collectors in the full knowledge that it is likely to be one of the most expensive pens they will ever purchase. Alfred Dunhill started out as a manufacturer and supplier of high-class motoring accessories in the 1890s in London's Euston Road. The business prospered in Edwardian London, moving to the fashionable St. James's area and expanding the range of luxury goods for gentlemen. Over the years Dunhill's luggage and travel goods, cigars, and lighters have been joined by wrist-watches, fountain pens, and writing accessories, while more recently fashion, fragrances, and jewelry have been offered to the international gentleman, all following Alfred Dunhill's maxim:

It must be useful,
It must work dependably,
It must be beautiful,
It must last,
It must be the best of its kind.

This maxim reached its finest expression during the 1930s in the Dunhill-Namiki pen, reputedly the only product sold by Dunhill which was not marketed exclusively under the Alfred Dunhill brand name until the purchase of Montblanc in 1985.

The Dunhill-Namiki was a perfect meeting of East and West. The ebonite fountain pen had been imported into Japan from the West in the 1880s but was prone to fading. In 1925 Ryosuke Namiki had the idea of painting their barrels with traditional lacquer, a natural varnish, which once dried is almost impenetrable and renders the pen barrel impervious to chemicals and salt, heat, and water. It was not long before another traditional technique followed and the ancient art and craft of *Maki-e* was transferred to pens. *Maki-e* was developed more than 1,500 years ago, and is the painstaking decoration of lacquerware with powdered gold and silver, flakes of gold, or mother-of-pearl and seashells.

MAKI-E PROCESS

Maki-e was originally used to decorate ornaments for the Japanese nobility, and was first applied to pens in the mid 1920s. There are three main types of Maki-e: Hira-maki-e, or flat lacquerwork; Togidashi-maki-e, or clouded and burnished lacquer work; Taka-maki-e, or raised and embossed lacquerwork with a three-dimensional effect when finished. The majority of quality Maki-e work uses gold dust. To decorate a pen the original design is transferred from the paper onto the pen surface in lacquer. Powdered gold or silver or colored pigments are applied to the drawing before the lacquer has dried, then clear lacquer is applied to seal the gold or silver powder. Next the background is painted with black lacquer or dusted with gold or silver dust to create the effect of landscape or atmospheric effects such as mist. Gradually the delicate design is built up by alternately applying lacquer and gold or silver. Between applications the lacquer surface is polished and buffed with charcoal until the gold dust is visible once again. Finally, when the design is completed, the whole surface is burnished repeatedly with special oil and whetting powders until the unique luster of Maki-e is achieved. The entire process takes many weeks.

A limited edition of 200 Alfred Dunhill-Namiki Maki-e pens. Traditionally, quail was kept as a domestic fowl in the East. It is balanced by the balloon and spear flowers, indigenous to Japan.

In 1926 the Namiki Manufacturing Co. opened branches in New York, London, Shanghai, and Singapore. The London manager was Setsuji Wada, son of Masao Wada, Namiki's business partner. Some examples of these pens may be found under the Namiki brand name or under those of luxury stores such as Asprey. Alfred Dunhill was quick to see their potential. He obtained the agency to sell them in France and in 1930 signed a contract to cover the European and American markets. An agreement was reached between the two firms, each proud of their name, that the pens would be marketed as "Dunhill-Namiki Made in Japan." It is believed that the contract expired at the beginning of World War II.

COMPANY FACTS

EST. First pen late 1920s

London, England

Pilot Pens, Japan

Dunhill branches worldwide

$ ★ ★ ★ ★

A very rare set of four Dunhill-Namiki conical Maki-e *bridge pencils made in the early 1930s. Each has a different decoration, from left to right:* Tatsuno Otoshigo *(seahorse),* Tai-fish *(sea-bream),* Medaka *(a Japanese freshwater fish), and* Kamo *(goose).*

Dunhill-Namiki marketed a wide range of products. Their pens ranged in size from the tiny #1 to the giant #50. Several pencils were also made, as well as desk sets, clocks, and the now famous Dunhill lighter. It is not widely known that celluloid Dunhill-Namiki pens were also produced, but to judge by their enormous scarcity today these were probably made in small numbers. Custom *Maki-e* orders were also undertaken, and the Dunhill Museum is a haven for a wide range of everyday objects transformed into works of art by *Maki-e*. Dunhill catalogs show that five standards of work were available:

C   Plain lacquer
B   Standard
A   Top-quality raised lacquer
AA   Top-quality gold-raised lacquer
AAA The finest quality

For Western eyes the work was a revelation. Namiki had employed Gonroku Matsuda, an important Japanese artist, to create the original designs and a school of 30 of his pupils calling themselves the Kokko-kai worked in the Namiki factory. Gonroku Matsuda has since received the accolade of "Living National Treasure" in Japan and been awarded the Order of Cultural Merit. His pupils have created the relaunched Alfred Dunhill-Namiki.

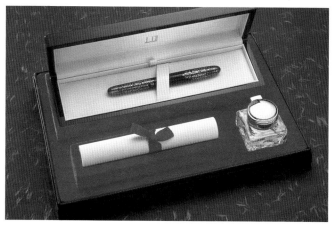

When presented individually, each Alfred Dunhill-Namiki pen comes in an ash wood case, together with a numbered certificate and a crystal inkwell.

SILVER NAMIKI

A rare silver and lacquer Dunhill-Namiki pen c.1928. This is decorated with orange and green sunflowers, red chrysanthemums, and gold leaf clover in the cloisonné style.

CRANE AND PINE TREE

A limited edition of 200 Alfred Dunhill-Namiki Maki-e pens. The Crane and the Pine Tree are two of the Ten Longevities symbolizing all the blessings of a long and healthy life and even immortality. These symbols can be depicted singly or in any combination.

HARE'S FOOT FERN

A limited edition of 200 Alfred Dunhill-Namiki Maki-e pens. The hare's foot fern is a popular ornamental plant in Japan and owes its name to its extraordinary aerial roots which appear to be covered with fur. The motif from nature has been semiabstracted by the Maki-e artist to create a delicate and intricate design. Each "frond" has been painstakingly delineated in silver and the dew drops which tremble on the leaves are actually created from tiny fragments of iridescent abalone shell. The skill of the artist is judged by the way in which the spirit or essence of the subject is captured.

RAKUCHO

A limited edition of 100 Alfred Dunhill-Namiki Maki-e pens. An ancient figure of uncertain origin, the Rakucho is a mythical bird, possibly related to the Phoenix. The Rakucho symbolizes a "peaceful atmosphere in heaven." In Oriental philosophy the idea of heaven differs from that of the West: Eastern religions affirm nature and the universe, and the state for which one must strive is a unity of nature and man—harmony with the universal life-spirit. On this pen the Rakucho perches amidst cherry blossoms, which are the national flowers of Japan and represent the transience of man's existence.

CRANE & PINE TREE

HARE'S FOOT FERN

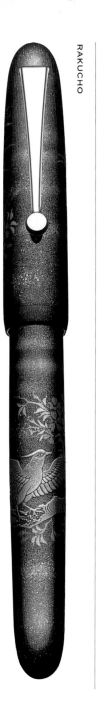

RAKUCHO

MAKI-E RADEN PEN

Over the years Alfred Dunhill has been inundated with inquiries from collectors wanting to know when another Dunhill-Namiki pen would be made. The answer came in early 1996 when a collection of four limited-edition Alfred Dunhill-Namiki pens was unveiled, and described by Mark Dunhill as "an important chapter in the 70-year history of Dunhill writing instruments, offering exclusive, exciting, and rare objects for discerning customers." Each of these pens is crafted by hand, taking more than three months to complete, and involving as many as 80 different processes. The design of each is unique and should be regarded as a three-dimensional painting. Each is decorated with a traditional Japanese design, often a stylized version of nature, with a symbolic meaning. Three of the pens are an edition of 200, while only 100 Rakucho were made. Twenty-eight sets of all four pens were produced in a hand-crafted black lacquered wood writing cabinet, containing a crystal inkwell and special writing paper.

COMPANY PRODUCTS

Known for the exclusive *Maki-e* lacquer pen, the

ALFRED DUNHILL-NAMIKI

A superb Maki-e Raden ladies' pen decorated with nine-stick fans on a red lacquer ground sprinkled with aogai, c.1926–30. This is one of the finest examples of the time consuming work that went into making the very best Maki-e pens.

Aurora

AURORA IS A GIANT of the Italian pen industry and in recent years has come to occupy a well-deserved place on the world stage too. Historically, the company has followed the guidelines of the world market established by the giant American companies, while continuing to be competitive, to contribute original technical research, and manufacture original products.

The company's roots can be traced to Isaia Levi, a Turin textile merchant, who in 1919 invested in the development of an Italian fountain pen. The name chosen for his *Fabbrica Italiana Penne a Serbatoio* was "Aurora", and production commenced at Via Basilica 9. The designs of the early pens were similar to those of Waterman who had a strong presence in Italy at the time, and whose pens had been brought back to Italy by troops returning from World War I. The first two models were both made in hard rubber, the eye-dropper F.A. (Fisso-Aurora) and eye-dropper safety R.A. (Rientrante-Aurora). The first years cannot have been easy for Aurora as they were only one of several competing enterprises established after World War I to try and build a native Italian pen manufacturing industry. Aurora seem to have had the edge in their advertising and their competitive pricing, however, which is still the case today.

One of the many imaginative campaigns used by Aurora.

DANTE ALIGHIERI

The Dante Alighieri limited edition was released to commemorate Aurora's 75th anniversary in 1994. Dante (1265–1321), Italy's most famous poet, experienced the cultural and political battles marking the passage of the Middle Ages into the Renaissance. His Divine Comedy *inspired Aurora to make a divine pen in green lacquer, decorated with vermeil trim with period engraving and a portrait of the poet. Two editions of 1919 pens were produced, one for the world market, the other for the Italian. Each was sold with an inkpot, booklet, and wooden case.*

88 FOUNTAIN PEN

The Aurora 88 was designed in 1946 in association with Marcello Nizzoli. It was redesigned in the 1980s with the present open nib replacing the original hooded nib. The pen now has a hidden ink-reservoir which allows it to continue writing for almost a page after the tank appears to have run dry. It is available as a fountain pen, rollerball, ballpoint, and pencil in black, classic with gold-plated cap.

DANTE ALIGHIERI

88 FOUNTAIN PEN

*The Jewelry Collection is Aurora's premium
line offering the 88 in a range of precious metal finishes.*

One of Aurora's most powerful advertising campaigns took place in 1924. The advertising copy read "Every fountain pen imported from abroad represents a genuine gold coin which leaves Italy, and one day of unemployment for an Italian worker. Aurora is the Italian pen." This was supported in parliament by O. Belluzzo, who made a speech declaring: "Those who purchase abroad what is also produced in Italy betray the national economy." To this day Italian collectors are fiercely loyal to Aurora, still regarding it as their own pen manufacturer. In the late 1920s Aurora responded to imports of giant brightly-colored American pens by launching their own range of large Duplex pens in colored celluloid using a traditional lever-filling system.

Both the manufacturing and commercial sides of the company were completely restructured in 1925. Visits to Germany and the United States enabled Isaia Levi to learn from the experience of other companies and to apply this knowledge to Aurora. Sales were increased through a network of regular distributors, specialist shops, and stationers and two new trademarks, OLO and ASCO, were created. OLO was sold exclusively by newspaper shops, and in stations, at a price lower than that of competitive products. ASCO was aimed solely at those companies which used the fountain pen as a regular means of advertising. FIAT, the Italian car factory also based in Turin, and the CTI (the Italian Touring Club) were among the first organizations to commission special pens from Aurora. It is interesting to note that Aurora had already adopted the marketing strategies we are familiar with today, diversifying between trademarks and production lines in order to reach different areas of the market, and it was one of the first companies to introduce the fountain pen as a refined object suitable for corporate gifts.

COMPANY PRODUCTS

Known for quality pens for the medium- to high-price band

88 FOUNTAIN PEN
OPTIMA AUTORIDE
IPSILON
MAGELLANO
HASTIL
THESI
VARIOUS LIMITED EDITIONS

NIBS: varies between models, maximum 4: extra fine, fine, medium, broad.

INKS: range

OPTIMA AUROLIDE

IPSILON

OPTIMA AUROLIDE

The Aurora Optima has a distinctive 1930s silhouette and is produced in Auroloid, a material similar to celluloid. It is available as fountain pen or ballpoint in seven colors; the marbled cobalt blue, amber brown, emerald green, and gray smoke, as well as the solid colors of black, burgundy, and green. The pens are all piston fillers with a hidden ink-reservoir.

IPSILON

The Aurora Ipsilon is typically Italian in style. It is available in fountain pen, ballpoint, and rollerball in four colors; sea green, burgundy, and sunny yellow. It is a budget-range pen with a gold-plated nib.

The 1930s were a decade of great innovation for Aurora. The Novum range was launched in rounded and faceted versions with an important revolutionary filling system using a lever in the end. It also featured a safety clip with a sprung grip which guarded against theft and secured the pen to a pocket. The Asterotype series of 1934 was another revolutionary pen which could be operated with only one hand, as a slider on the barrel allowed the nib to be extended beyond a hinged cover. It is extremely rare and prized today and shares some features with the Pullman pen (see Yard-O-Led pp.182–184).

Another legendary pen of this era is the Etiopia, today shrouded in myth and apocryphal stories by collectors. The design, which became known as "The Empire Pen," celebrated the Italian acquisition of the Ethiopian Empire in the 1940s. The Etiopia is considered an important and unusual design today but it was not an enormous success at the time. Stocks were often converted into button-fillers and given to pharmaceutical companies as gifts for doctors. It is not widely known that the Etiopia was also available in red, green, and purple-gray.

MAGELLANO

The Magellano is one of Aurora's most recent designs. It is a more slender design than their 1980s and 90s pens and the collection is available as fountain pen, rollerball, and ballpoint in seven finishes; vermeil, sterling silver with either sterling-silver or gold-plated trim, black lacquer with vermeil cap, and three lacquers: blue, green, and burgundy.

Aurora had to rebuild their business and their factory after World War II, moving to Strada Abbadia di Stura, just outside Turin. Their postwar production includes numerous classic lines

AURORA

produced in association with leading designers. It is a curious feature of the fountain pen industry during these difficult times that those companies which brought in outside designers prospered, whereas those that did not frequently slipped into a terminal decline.

The Aurora 88 was a landmark for the company. Designed by Marcello Nizzoli, one of the masters of industrial design, it had a fashionable hooded nib and was introduced to combat the success of the Parker 51. Between 1947 and 1952 one million Aurora 88s had been made, sold under the slogan "bella e fedele" (beautiful and faithful). Albe Steiner was the next in a long series of famous designers to work with Aurora, designing the Sele ballpoint and Duocart Junior and winning Aurora the Golden Compass award in 1954. In 1963 the 98 Magic Reserve Pen was presented for the first time, having a special device which ensured a small ink reserve when the main tank ran out.

The Aurora Thesi ballpoint was a
collaboration between the Aurora style department
and Marco Zanuso. Like the Hastil, it has been
exhibited at MOMA.

*The Carlo Goldoni limited edition was named after the
great eighteenth-century Venetian playwright (1707–1793)
who made the Commedia dell' Arte famous worldwide. It
is the first of the Theater Series of limited editions, and is
made of solid silver decorated with the masks of comedy on
the band and packaged in a theater-shaped box. It was
released in 1993 as a dual edition of 1,793 pieces
worldwide, and another 1,793 for the Italian market.*

Lasting worldwide fame came to Aurora as a result of their
collaboration with Marco Zanuso which produced the Hastil
pen, the world's only fountain pen to be exhibited permanently
at MOMA, the Museum of Modern Art in New York. The
simple smooth line of this cylindrical pen made from ecosteel
has spawned many imitations. The advertising campaign used at
the time was so effective that sales rose dramatically as the
design-conscious Italian public besieged shops just to be able to
gaze at this wonderful new object. The Thesi and Hastil
ballpoints developed from further Aurora-Zanuso collaborations. The Marco Polo and Kona models followed in
subsequent years.

Aurora is now headed by Ing. Franco Verona, whose son Dott. Cesare Verona is a tireless ambassador for the company. They are widely respected for their innovative designs, Italian craftsmanship, and the style of their pens. Many examples in their current range look set for lengthy production runs and

COMPANY FACTS

Est. 1919

🏢 Turin, Italy

🏭 Turin, Italy

🚚 Widespread

$ ★ ★ to ★ ★ ★ ★

classic status in the future, while their limited-edition pens have a dedicated following throughout the world. Aurora has such strong and loyal support in Italy that it has to make two limited editions of each series to prevent the Italian domestic market ordering every single pen produced. Unlike some companies, Aurora sees the limited edition sector as an adjunct to its main business, and concentrates its main efforts on developing and marketing its extensive range of pens which covers the needs of the mid- to high-priced market.

The two men currently behind the running of Aurora;
Cesare Verona, on the left, with his father and head of
the company, Ing. Franco Verona.

Aurora released two different limited-edition pens to celebrate their 75th anniversary. The first was a gold-plated pen decorated with silver Art Nouveau rings recreating the Aurora pens of the 1920s. The other anniversary set (above) was a red fountain pen and ballpoint Optima.

Initially made in ivory-white celluloid, the Etiopia was filled with ink granules kept in a compartment at the end of the pen which were then dissolved in water. It had an imperial eagle on the cap and was used by Italian troops during the African wars where the intense heat would dry out normal ink.

Bexley Pen

THE BEXLEY PEN COMPANY was organized in 1993 and is run by a group of professional enthusiasts, producing a select range of pens. The founding members of the company have more than 40 years' experience in precision manufacturing, and more than 50 years' combined experience in collecting and dealing with fountain pens. They include the prominent vintage pen collector Howard Levy and L. Michael Fultz who also makes his own range of pens (see pp.104–107). This combination of experience with writing instruments and manufacturing has led to a range of products designed to appeal to both collectors and writers. The idea for each pen is a vintage design which gives a strong retro-feel, but it is then transformed by the use of modern acrylic, and tempered by the use of oldfashioned button-filling mechanisms.

The Bexley Giant is an oversized pen looselybased on the Parker Giant pen from the early years of the twentieth century. Made from durable cast acrylic in limited colors, it has an aerometric filling system. Each is a numbered edition of 100 pens with 10-ct. clips and flexible 14-ct. gold nibs.

THE BEXLEY ORIGINAL

The limited-edition Bexley Pen was produced in 1993. It is a classic bandless design reminiscent of the 1920s and 1930s. They were handmade from cast acrylic, which has an extremely durable finish and captures the look of shimmering crushed velvet. One hundred pens were made in each of four colors; green, burgundy, gray, and bronze. They are button-fillers and have medium-width flexible 14-ct. gold nibs.

CABLETWIST

The Bexley Cabletwist is a unique design on the market today. Companies such as Parker and Waterman made cable-twist hard rubber pens in the 1890s, but Bexley are the only company to look this far back for a design to develop. There are two designs of this tactile pen and three colors. The pen is a button-filler with a medium nib. There is also a matching rollerball.

BEXLEY DELUXE

BEXLEY DELUXE

The numbered edition of the Bexley Deluxe recalls the style of the Parker Lucky-Curve Duofold of the early 1920s. It is a full-size pen available in orange with black accents, or cream with woodgrain accents. Each has a wide 10-ct. gold band and a matching 10-ct. gold clip. It is a button-filler with a medium-width 14-ct. gold flexible nib.

COMPANY FACTS

EST. 1993

Columbus, Ohio
43204, USA

Entirely U.S.-made

From above

$ ★ ★ to ★ ★ ★

COMPANY PRODUCTS

Known for short-run limited editions

BEXLEY GIANT
THE BEXLEY ORIGINAL
CABLETWIST
BEXLEY DELUXE
EQUIPOISE

NIBS: medium-flexible as standard

Caran D'Ache

CARAN D'ACHE IS PROBABLY best-known for its first-class color products for drawing and painting which are used by some of the world's most famous artists. It also makes writing instruments in the same tradition of Swiss quality that has found expression in the Swiss watch industry.

Caran D'Ache has been based in Geneva since it was established in 1924 and is Switzerland's sole, exclusive pencil and writing instrument manufacturer. The firm's origins as manufacturers of artist's materials is revealed by the name they chose—Caran D'Ache means pencil in Russian and was the pen-name of the famous Belle Epoque caricaturist Emmanuel Poiré (1858–1909).

In 1974 Caran D'Ache introduced their prestige range of writing instruments, exclusive lighters, and leather accessories with the launching of the Madison or "Epée" Collection, the nickname derived from the distinctive sword clip which has become a signature for Caran D'Ache writing instruments. The Hexagonal Collection followed in 1980, finished in Chinese lacquer. The range of pens offered has widened over the last two decades and an annual series of limited editions aimed at the collectors' market was launched in 1995. A collectors' club for limited edition pens is due to be established soon.

The Geneva Collection is Caran D'Ache's top regular line and comprises fountain pen, ballpoint, pencil, and rollerball. Each is available in a range of Chinese lacquer finishes; black, "écaille," green, and blue. There is also a two-tone collection with metal caps.

Special orders of pens can be designed and made on a private-label basis. The team of in-house designers has created a triangular-shaped ballpoint for Bulgari, as well as supplying Tiffany, Rolls Royce, and Mercedes Benz who ordered a Geneva in a special color.

The Guinness Book of Records has two entries for Caran D'Ache writing instruments. The Madison ballpoint pen is the slimmest pen set with 684 diamonds in gold, and in 1995 a Geneva pen set with 4,255 diamonds became the most expensive pen in the world when it was sold for $120,500. Environmental protection is a very important issue in Switzerland and Caran D'Ache choose only raw materials that can be recycled. Their lacquer finishes are derived from the sap of the Asian sumac *Rhus verniciflua*, which is a renewable resource. Even their packaging comes complete with recycling instructions.

COMPANY FACTS

EST. 1924

Thonex-Geneva, Switzerland

Thonex-Geneva, Switzerland

Worldwide except for certain African countries

$ ★ to ★ ★ ★ ★

COMPANY PRODUCTS

Known for prestige, lifestyle, office, and collectors' pens, inks, pouches, boxes, artist's materials, etc.

MADISON
HEXAGONAL COLLECTION
GENEVA
PRIVATE COLLECTION
LA MODERNISTA
LIMITED EDITIONS
CUSTOM ORDERS
LADY
ECRIDOR

NIBS: six: extra-fine, fine, medium, broad, medium-oblique, medium-broad

INKS: bottles and cartridges

MADISON

HEXAGONAL COLLECTION

PRIVATE COLLECTION

LA MODERNISTA

MADISON

The lacquer Madison Collection was first made in 1974 and is affectionately nicknamed L'Epée, a reference to the distinctive sword-shaped clip. The fountain pen, ballpoint, roller pen, and pencil are available in four marble lacquers designed to look luxurious, but provide a color-coordinating range of accessories at a reasonable price.

HEXAGONAL COLLECTION

The Hexagonal Collection is one of Caran D'Ache's popular lines, available with matching lighter, ballpoint, pencil, and rollerball. The Chinese lacquer finish is applied by hand, and accentuates the geometry of the pen's shape.

PRIVATE COLLECTION

Caran D'Ache celebrated their 70th anniversary in 1994 with the launch of their first limited edition of Collection Privée. It was available as a set of fountain pen and matching ballpoint with matching numbers, each an edition of 2,000 pieces.

LA MODERNISTA

La Modernista is the second edition of Caran D'Ache's private collection. The limited-edition size of 1,888 pieces was chosen because the 1888 World's Fair in Barcelona heralded the birth of Modernism. This is comparable with Art Nouveau in France, Jugendstil in Germany, and Liberty in England and characterized by exotic designs and polychrome mosaics. The Modernist movement saw collaborations between artists, craftsmen, and designers; Caran D'Ache's La Modernista has brought together silversmiths, jewelers, enamelers, and glass artists. The pen is presented with a crystal inkwell designed by Lluis Ventós in a shell form which echoes the organic references in the pen.

Cartier

Cartier is probably the most prestigious jeweler in the world today. Fountain pens are only a small part of their business but are as distinctive as many other Cartier products, such as wrist watches, for which the company is famous throughout the world.

Maison Cartier was born in 1847 when Louis-François Cartier (1819–1904) followed Maître Adolphe Picard in taking over his jewelry workshop at 31 rue Montorgueil in Paris. Six years later, in 1853, Cartier started undertaking work for private clients and the house flourished during the opulent Second Empire under Napoleon III. The Empress Eugénie was a valued patron, and Louis-François Cartier's friendship with the famous couturier Worth was also to benefit his workshops.

This magnificent late-seventeenth century Mugal
emerald was mounted as a pendant brooch by Cartier
c.1915. The setting is typical of the "white jewelry" for
which Cartier achieved world fame.

LOUIS CARTIER

Cartier's son Alfred (1841–1925) took over the business in 1874 and introduced the first bracelet watch in 1888. His success enabled Cartier to move to a prestigious new premises at 13 rue de la Paix, where the company remains to this day. Alfred entrusted his three sons with the international future of Maison Cartier. Louis-Joseph (1875–1942) took over responsibility in Paris, Jacques-Théodule (1884–1942) established himself in London and Pierre-Camille (1878–1964) went to New York.

The three brothers spread the reputation of Cartier as the most prestigious jeweler in the world. They were awarded Royal Warrants from more than a dozen countries and traveled widely to develop their business. They rivaled Peter Carl Fabergé for commissions from the phenomenally wealthy aristocrats of pre-revolutionary Russia, reset the Maharajah's treasures in the latest styles created in the Cartier studios in London, and cultivated clients from finance and modern industry in the New World including the Rockefeller, Vanderbilt, Gould, and Ford families.

LOUIS CARTIER

The most recent addition to the range. Named after the most dynamic member of the Cartier family, and reflecting the ongoing Cartier heritage — the Cartier Museum has a vintage Cartier pen in fluted gold with a sapphire cabochon on the top.

PANTHÈRE

Available in fountain pen and ballpoint versions, the Panthère was first produced in 1991. A combination of gold and enamel it bears the three gold rings of the Cartier trademark.

COUGAR PEN

The "brother" of the Panthère pen. The cap is set with an onyx cabochon and the trademark three gold rings are around the middle of the godron-striped body. Available in fountain pen and ballpoint.

Cartier embraced the Art Nouveau and Art Deco movements with whole-hearted enthusiasm, revolutionized the art of jewelry and created a widespread demand for luxury objects and accessories. The Santos-Dumont bracelet watch (named after the pioneering Brazilian aviator) and the "Tank" wristwatch were bought

COMPANY FACTS	
Est.	1847
🏢	Paris, France
🏭	Paris, France
🚚	Worldwide from Cartier agents
$	★ ★ ★

throughout the world. The creation of the "S" department (S for Silver) in 1923 is regarded by Cartier today as the first step toward democratization of the jeweler, and the precursor of Must de Cartier.

The first line of Hardstone pens was launched by Cartier in 1924, made of onyx, moonstone, and opal. It was a success and pens were ordered by famous writers including Francis de Croisset, Sacha Guitry, and Paul Claudel. The Maharajah of Kapurthala ordered several. These were not the first pens made by Cartier as their archive includes a fountain pen made c.1910, as well as other writing instruments from before this time, but it was probably the first time Cartier marketed a range of pens en masse.

The Cartier that many people would recognize today was created during the late 1960s and the 1970s under the leadership of Robert Hocq, a man who had been fascinated by Cartier. He licensed a luxury gas cigarette lighter under the Cartier name in 1968, and became chairman of Cartier Paris in 1972 when it came under the control of investors brought together by Joseph Kanoui. Hocq and Alain-Dominique Perrin developed new ranges and Les Must de Cartier lines, opening concessions in centers of "new money" around the world, especially in the Far East. At the same time Kanoui and his investors bought Cartier London in 1974 and Cartier New York in 1976, finally reuniting the company as Cartier Monde in 1979. Cartier has been part of the Vendôme Luxury Group since October 1993, an umbrella company which combines Cartier, Alfred Dunhill, Montblanc, Piaget, Baume & Mercier, Karl Lagerfeld, Chloe, Sulka, Hackett, and Seeger.

The Must de Cartier line is probably the most instantly recognizable of Cartier fountain pens, popular since the late 1970s.

COMPANY PRODUCTS

Known for quality pens for an international market

LOUIS CARTIER
PANTHÈRE
COUGAR PEN
MUST DE CARTIER

Custom pens and presentation pens

Today's Cartier pens echo aspects of the Cartier heritage in particular the three-hoop ring in three colors of gold first introduced in 1924. This is used as a signature on many Cartier pens today. Cartier progressed from the Art Deco style to a return to nature, and the renowned panthers and tigers of their jewelry, for which the most famous clients were the Duchess of Windsor, Barbara Hutton, and Nina Dyer is repeated in the Panthère and Cougar pens. Pens are developed in France, where product trials are also carried out, then released simultaneously worldwide.

The latest Cartier pen, the Stylo Louis Cartier, returns to a more conventional design than some recent pens—particularly the top-heavy Pasha and the oval Must. As you would expect from a jeweler of Cartier's reputation it is possible to order a bespoke pen in any combination of precious metals and gemstones. Cartier also pride themselves on their presentation pens, suitably engraved and adorned.

The recently designed Stylo Louis Cartier is available in several finishes, but also made to order if requested.

Classic Pens

CLASSIC PENS WAS ESTABLISHED in 1987, specializing in the repair and sale of vintage and modern fountain pens, and launched the first of an exclusive series of CP pens in 1990. The company is run by Andreas Lambrou, who started to collect pens at the age of 12. Andy moved to England to study science in 1961, and continued to add to his collection during his 21 years in the food flavor industry from 1965–1986. He is the proud co-owner of two patents from this time, one of which is for a novel onion flavor found in many house-hold foods.

In 1987 Andy and his wife Jenny took the bold step of giving up their jobs to devote themselves full-time to their love of pens, writing *Fountain Pens Vintage and Modern* and establishing Classic Pens Ltd. The book quickly came to be regarded as the definitive work on the history of fountain pens and their industry and has since been published in five languages.

COMPANY FACTS

EST. 1987

Essex, England

Varies, depending on source of pen

Best to order direct from Classic Pens (see Resource Guide)

$ ★ ★ ★

Many collectors of vintage pens were surprised when Classic Pens announced their first limited-edition pen in 1990. At this point people were discovering the heritage of the fountain pen for the first time and, intent on concentrating on the past, could not understand the direction the Lambrous and their partner Keith Brown were taking. What Classic Pens had done, however, was to realize that just as some people eschew vintage automobiles in favor of modern cars, not everyone necessarily wants to use a vintage pen.

Classic Pens' CP series was intended to offer pen lovers a unique collection of quality pens exclusively manufactured by the leading pen companies in a limited edition which would not be available elsewhere. The first pen—CP1-Targa by Sheaffer— was offered in an edition of 250 sterling silver pens in a rich "vannerie" pattern and presented in an exclusive handmade box.

CP2 Pushkin was launched in 1993 and was a limited edition of 500 Sheaffer Crest pens, again in sterling silver. A collaboration between Classic Pens, Sheaffer, and Pushkin Prizes, this celebrated the famous 19th-century Russian poet.

By 1995 the CP brand name was much stronger and production was increased to 1,000 pieces as CP3 was issued as a twin edition of 500 Homer Iliad and 500 Homer Odyssey pens. The pens were in sterling silver, this time the 88 made by the prestigious Italian pen company Aurora (see pp. 55–64). The 88 was designed by acclaimed industrial architect Marcello Nizzoli and first made in 1947. It featured a refined piston-filling mechanism, and an advanced feed which facilitated improved and regular ink flow. The large 88 used by Classic Pens

The Iliad (top) and the Odyssey are presented in hand-crafted cases, made exclusively for them.

CP1-TARGA

incorporates an ingenious hidden reservoir system which allows the pen to continue writing for at least another page after the ink has apparently run dry. It is the first time this pen has been offered entirely in sterling silver. The two guilloche engravings, diamond Iliad and flammé Odyssey, were created and applied specifically by the Murelli company in France.

Classic Pens' policy of marketing exclusive editions of a quality pen has paid off. The pens chosen all have a worldwide reputation for reliability, and appeal to collectors of a particular marque as well as of the CP series. Following the publication of their second book *Fountain Pens of the World* in 1995, the Lambrous put up their collection of vintage pens for auction and set several world record prices.

Classic Pens have been listening to their customers' suggestions, and a new pen is in development. This will be a deluxe model, having a more elaborate finish, a two-tone nib, and redesigned packaging. It will have no manufacturer's logo and will be the first pen to be sold exclusively under the CP brand.

COMPANY PRODUCTS

Known for limited editions of pens
exclusively manufactured
by international pen companies

CP1
CP2
CP3

NIBS: six: extra-fine, fine, medium, broad,
medium-oblique, stub

CP2-PUSHKIN

CP3-ODYSSEY

The Fountain Pen Directory

CP1-TARGA

The pen chosen for 1990s CP1 was the stylish Targa by Sheaffer, first launched in 1976 and now regarded as a modern classic.

CP2-PUSHKIN

The Sheaffer Crest was used for CP2 Pushkin in 1993. The cap is engraved with Pushkin's autograph and the last verse of his Autumn which refers to the inspiration of pen and paper.

CP3 PENS

The Aurora 88 CP3 Homer pens, named after the epic poems The Iliad and The Odyssey which are among the greatest works of world literature. The strength and purity of the diamond-design Iliad (shown on page 79) was chosen to reflect the Greek hero Achilles, and the complexity and ingenuity of the Odyssey (shown here) symbolizes the resourcefulness of Odysseus (Ulysses) as he journeyed home from the Trojan war.

Columbus

COLUMBUS ARE ONE OF THE SMALLEST Italian pen companies, and are making pens again after a long period of decline. The business was established in 1918 by Alfredo and Eugenio Verga who wanted to make pens in Milan. Their earliest pens were strongly influenced by German design as they purchased the bulk of their parts and much of their raw materials from Germany. The first pen had been called Columbus, and this was the name selected when a trademark was finally registered on November 18, 1924. Shortly after this Columbus Extra was also registered and used for their top range of pens. The first incarnation of Columbus came to a halt soon after this, having failed to ride the fountain-pen boom of the early 1920s.

Eugenio Verga restarted the company under his own name in 1927. He patented a new feed in 1928 and a new filling system in 1929 and started to make pens to more modern designs from colorful celluloids. The company prospered but, in common with many other small Italian companies at the time, pen design was strongly influenced by American models. As followers rather than leaders they were unable to become

PRESTIGIO

*The Prestigio line was relaunched in 1994.
A utilitarian range available in a variety of finishes including gold and silver plate, lacquers, and chrome. A robust range which also meets the Italian desire for good industrial design.*

larger than regional or national concerns. The company was forced to move to Lesa on Lake Maggiore after the plant was destroyed in World War II, but returned to Milan in 1951 where the factory has remained at Via Trebbia 26 to this day.

The postwar decades brought uncertainty to Columbus. Eugenio Verga, who had guided the business through its prime, died in 1957, and the business passed to his son Enrico who was unable to maintain profitability in the face of the ballpoint and the declining popularity of the fountain pen.

Santara srl bought the Columbus trademark and factory in 1992 and are rebuilding production. Outside designers were brought in to create the Linea Accademia and Columbus are once more producing an attractive range of mid- and budget-priced pens for the Italian market. Traditional celluloid is used to make the Accademia, while the Versailles and Prestigio use metals and lacquer finishes.

Current plans call for a hand-assembled pen to be made to a design inspired by the 130 series of pens popular during the 1930s and 1940s. It is certain to be marketed almost entirely in Italy as an Italian pen and will appeal to consumers with a strong loyalty to a historic local marque. What will be interesting to watch is how Santara attempt to build on this solid base, and whether they decide to launch the third incarnation of Columbus into a wider arena.

COMPANY PRODUCTS

Known for mid-price and budget pens and writing instruments

PRESTIGIO
VERSAILLES
ACCADEMIA

NIBS: fine, medium, broad

INKS: range of colors; cartridges

VERSAILLES

ACCADEMIA

VERSAILLES

The Versailles line was introduced in 1993. Clean lines and strong, simple colors. Fine- or medium-nib pens, matching rollerball, pencil, and ballpoint.

ACCADEMIA

The Accademia line was introduced in 1993 and is available in a variety of patterns and marbled celluloids. Fine, medium, or broad nibs, fountain pen, and ballpoint.

A. T. Cross

AMERICA'S OLDEST MANUFACTURER of fine writing instruments, A.T. Cross was established in either New York or Providence, Rhode Island in the early 1840s. The exact date remains a mystery, as "Since 1846," part of the corporate logo, recognizes the birth of the company's namesake Alonzo Townsend Cross (1846–1922). However, some time before that Alonzo's father, Richard Cross, his uncle Benjamin Cross and Alonzo's stepgrandfather-in-law, Edward W. Bradbury, were making writing instruments and jewelry.

The Cross family came from England's so-called Black Country, just north of Birmingham. John Cross (1771–1835) was an agent and wharfinger for one of the earliest enterprises of the Industrial Revolution. It is uncertain how his sons became involved in the jewelry business and moved to New York.

Richard Cross married in New York in 1844, but soon returned to England perhaps to seek the skilled craftsmen and tools he brought back to Boston during 1847. He then made pens and pencil cases in gold and silver. In 1850 he established a relatively large concern with 12 employees in Attleborough, Massachusetts, and after the great financial panic of 1857 he moved into Bradbury's workshop in nearby Providence, Rhode Island.

By the end of the American Civil War the company had tripled in size. A.T. Cross had joined his father at an early age and was made a partner in 1871. By the end of his career A.T. Cross had been personally granted 25 patents for writing instruments, including five for fountain pens, nine for stylographic pens, a further three for a combination of stylographic and fountain pens, six for pencils, one for a nib holder, and one for a method of enameling or japanning hollow articles.

COMPANY FACTS	
EST.	1840s
🏢	Lincoln, Rhode Island, U.S.A.
🏭	Lincoln, Rhode Island, U.S.A. Ballinasloe, County Galway, Ireland (Manufacturers for Europe, Middle East, Africa)
🚚	Worldwide
$	★ to ★ ★ ★ ★

During the 1870s A.T. Cross had two major projects in hand. He collaborated with Stillman Saunders to develop a steam engine which he applied to his workshop and the production of writing instruments. By 1896 he had built a carriage around it, creating and driving the first automobile in Providence. However, the stylographic pen is often regarded as A.T.'s greatest achievement. It revolutionized fountain pens and the art of correspondence as a whole. It was the first successful writing instrument

COMPANY PRODUCTS

Known for a wide range of writing instruments. Strong tradition of decorating pens with corporate logos

TOWNSEND COLLECTION
METROPOLIS COLLECTION
SOLO COLLECTION
VARIOUS LIMITED EDITIONS

NIBS: extra-fine, fine, medium, broad

INKS: bottles: limited range of colors; cartridges

TOWNSEND COLLECTION

The Townsend Collection is top of the current Cross range and named after Alonzo Townsend Cross. It marks a move away from the traditional slim shape of Cross products over the last half century, and was an important development for the firm as larger pens are in demand today. It comprises fountain pen, pencil, rollerball, and ballpoint, each available in lapis lazuli, gold-plate, titanium, lacquer, and medalist (two-tone metal) finishes. The design is derived from the Art Deco Cross pen of the 1930s.

that could produce an ink-written original with multiple carbon copies. It delivered wet ink to paper through a strong tubular needle and spindle that served as a writing point in place of the traditional nib. A writer could therefore bear down hard enough to write through carbons. Prior to this invention carbon copies could only be made with pencil because the traditional nib was too soft and flexible to bear the necessary pressure without breaking. The stylographic pen was so important an invention that the U.S. Post Office almost immediately made its use mandatory.

*The Solo Collection is a budget line using
traditional Cross styling and is available in four
"European" colors.*

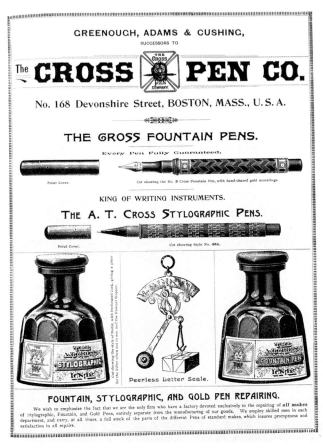

This trade catalog from 1892 illustrates a Cross fountain pen, a Cross stylographic pen, the Cross ink bottle, and letter scale.

The company made fountain pens for much of its long history, although this is little known today, and from 1881 to the second decade of this century there was a Cross Pen Company alongside the A.T. Cross Pencil Company. In 1916 A.T. Cross sold his company to Walter Russell Boss Sr. who had worked as a salesman for the company. A.T. Cross has remained a family concern, and today brothers Bradford R. Boss and Russell A. Boss serve as Chairman and President respectively.

The most famous Cross pen was made during the 1930s. It was a handsome, large pen available in gold-filled or chrome metal, decorated with black enamel bands. It seems to have been made in small quantities, possibly because Cross had accepted a quantity of mechanisms from the bankrupt LeBoeuf company in order to discharge a debt. It was advertised as a supporting product to the Cross pencil (rather than the other way around) and was discontinued around 1940. Its classic Art Deco silhouette has been the mainstay of Cross fountain pens since their reintroduction in 1982, and lends itself well to modern production.

The fountain pen was reintroduced after a 40-year gap during which it was assumed that the ballpoint, soft-tip, and rollerball pens would supplant the fountain pen. Cross had enjoyed

To celebrate their 150th anniversary, Cross made an individually-numbered limited edition of 10,000 replicas of their famous 1930s pen. The pen nib was engraved with a lion's head, based on an original Cross logo from the nineteenth century.

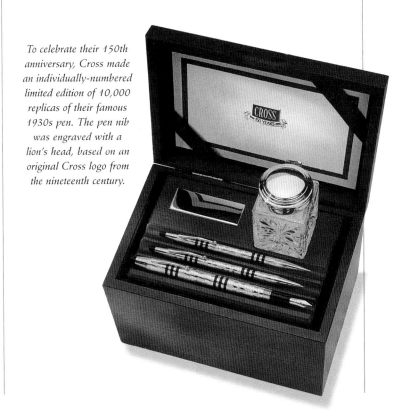

enormous success with all these products, and initially only reintroduced the pen to the export market. The nib tip is made of ruthenium and requires an initial wearing-in period before it can conform to the owner's handwriting style.

The manufacturing process for Cross writing instruments includes both machine- and hand-operations. None of their pens is completely handmade, and they do not suffer from the obsessive desire to produce a handmade product which is holding back many of the small- to medium-sized European companies. Their pens have a metal, usually brass, shell, which is then decorated with precious metal, European lacquers, or a titanium coating through a physical vapor-deposition process.

A.T. Cross have a longstanding tradition of customizing their product with a range of corporate logos.

METROPOLIS COLLECTION

The Metropolis Collection echoes the design of America's skyscrapers, and has a skyscraper skyline engraved on the nib. It was designed to appeal to progressive urban professionals and comprises fountain pen, pencil, rollerball, and ballpoint, each available in six finishes.

Diplomat

IPLOMAT IS A SMALL GERMAN COMPANY which intends to raise its low profile with a greater degree of specialization. It was founded in 1922 as Hennefer Schreibwarenfabrik Räuchle & Co. The first pens to be sold under the Diplomat brand name were made in 1950 and were inexpensive generic German pens. Diplomat was one of the first German companies to introduce the ink cartridge after the Jif-Waterman patent of 1953 had run out. The company had all but disappeared from view when it was acquired by the present owners in 1981 and became part of IMCO J. Michaelis in Stuttgart.

COMPANY FACTS	
EST.	1922
🏢	Stuttgart, Germany
🏭	Pforzheim, Baden Württemberg, Germany Cunewalde, Sachsen, Germany Hennef, Nordrhein Westfalen, Germany
🚚	Worldwide
$	★ ★

The Diplomat pen box includes a space for an ink bottle as well as pens and other utensils.

A new series of pens was introduced in the late 1980s and included Epoque, Attaché, Embassy, and Lord. The company now makes pens for other brands including an outdoor sports pen for Camel and a revived Kaweco company. Proprietary brands are an important part of the Diplomat business and they will make special orders of sterling-silver pens. Production time is around three months for the minimum order of 1,000 pieces. Diplomat specialize in nib production and special surfaces including rubber and lacquer. Their own pens are mainly designed in-house and are both handmade and machine-made.

COMPANY PRODUCTS

Known for proprietary brands and special orders

CLASSIC COLLECTION
BALANCE
ATTACHÉ
XL

NIBS: gold, steel

INKS: bottles

CLASSIC COLLECTION

The Diplomat Classic Collection is a range of traditional styled pens, ballpoints, and pencils. They are available in a number of finishes which include black lacquer, green, brown or blue-marbled lacquer, green or brown ebonite, and a blue-faceted version. The pens have an engraved steel nib.

BALANCE

ATTACHÉ

BALANCE

The Diplomat Balance Collection is a slender instrument available as fountain pen, ballpoint, pencil, and rollerball. The finishes include black, graphite, blue marble, sunset red, and midnight green lacquer, some of which are available with a gold-plated cap. An all-gold-plated version is also offered. The pen has an 18-ct. solid gold nib.

ATTACHÉ

The Attaché Collection was introduced in 1990 and is available as fountain pen, ballpoint, rollerball, and pencil. There are seven lacquer finishes; brown marble, green, black, burgundy, blue, aubergine, graphite, and racing green. Chrome is offered as an eighth choice. The pen has a gold-plated, two-color stainless-steel nib.

S. T. Dupont

S.T. DUPONT HAS ONE OF THE MOST UNUSUAL origins of any pen manufacturer today. François Tissot-Dupont was appointed official portrait photographer to the court of Emperor Napoleon III of France in 1846. He was joined by his nephew Simon Tissot-Dupont, who later took over his position. S.T. Dupont was also famous for producing high-quality leather goods for his patrons in addition to taking their photographs, and in 1872 he founded the company that still bears his name.

Simon's two sons, Lucien and André, joined the company and expanded the workshops at Faverges, a small town in Upper Savoy nestling in the foothills of the Alps. They added

COMPANY FACTS

Est. 1872

Paris, France

Faverges, Haute Savoie, France

Worldwide

$ ★ ★ to ★ ★ ★ ★

other skilled craftsmen to the now famous leather workers and continued the strategy of producing luxury items in small numbers until World War II put an end to this type of small craftsmanship. In 1939 the company developed the Dupont lighter from a smoker's accessory created for the Maharajah of Patiala's dressing case. S.T. Dupont diversified during the 1960s and extended its skills to other prestige products. The range now includes men's luxury ready-to-wear clothes and accessories from cigar-cutters to cufflinks.

S.T. Dupont are famous for their authentic Chinese lacquer-work which was added to their stable of craftsman metalworkers, engravers, and enamelers by accident. In 1937 when advertising for an *ouvrier plaqueur* (jewelry plater) their advert was misprinted as *ouvrier laqueur* and the firm was joined by a White Russian who had learned ancient Chinese skills while a prisoner in the Sino-Russian war. This technique is one of S.T. Dupont's trademarks today, and the method a jealously-guarded secret handed down from generation to generation within the company.

The lacquer workshop at Faverges is the only one closed to the public as the firm is secretive about the precise details of its

CHAIRMAN

CHAIRMAN

The Chairman, as its name implies, is the leading pen in Dupont's top range, Les Montparnasse. It was designed by Xavier Rousseau and introduced in 1989. The nib echoes the shape of a quill pen, and the line has an original system for unscrewing the barrel with a concealed semicircular handle similar to the Dupont lighter. Les Montparnasse comprises two sizes of fountain pen, ballpoint pen, and pencil and is offered in a variety of finishes. The Chairman is available in a natural (amber) translucent lacquer and the Chairman Garnet, introduced in 1993, in red.

COMPANY PRODUCTS

Known for ranges of middle and luxury market pens, custom pieces, business gifts, ink, leather cases, and accessories

LES MONTPARNASSE
LES OR MASSIF
LES PORTE-PLUME
LES CLASSIQUES
GATSBY
FIDELO
ANNUAL LIMITED EDITION

INKS: bottles and cartridges

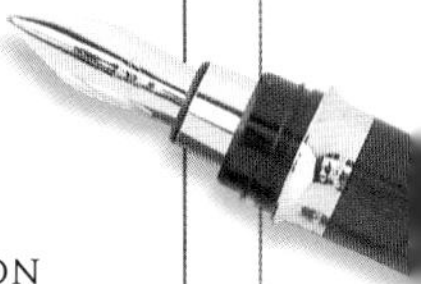

Les Elements limited editions were Dupont's interpretation of Earth, Water, Fire, and Air, and 200 pens were made for each element. There are four colors of translucent Chinese lacquer, brown with gold dust (Earth). Nile green (Water), flaming red stripes inset with gold (Fire), and sky blue (Air).

authentic Chinese lacquering process. Their lacquer is derived from the sap of the *Rhus vernicifera* tree in the Far East and sent direct to France. It is the complex and lengthy decanting, filtering, maturing, and coloring process which Dupont intends to keep secret. The process of applying and polishing lacquer layer by layer to give an amazing depth is much better known as it has been practiced in the Far East for more than 1,000 years.

The company launched its first pens in 1973 as accessories to its lighters. Today Dupont views pens as a major line and is continually developing collections—both limited editions and main ranges. They are firmly aimed at the mid and upper end of the market. Up to 140 processes are involved in making their pens, which are usually made from brass for strength and weight. Dupont also manufacture for other luxury brands including Hermes, Bulgari, and Louis Vuitton.

S.T. Dupont
PARIS

Dupont's reputation for quality, using the skills of traditional craftsmen, is an important part of their marketing strategy, but they are also helped by having some 6,000 sales points around the world. The product line ranges from solid gold pens and lacquer pens studded with diamonds, to the 1994 Fidelio range aimed at younger customers. Fidelio is brightly colored and the ballpen and pencils can be converted from one to another simply by changing the refill.

Great importance is attached by Dupont to the creation of limited editions and unique, custom-made pieces in keeping with their tradition of luxury master craftsmen. Royalty and heads of state are among their customers, but Dupont prefer not to trade on their names, believing that exporting 80% of production is sufficient worldwide recognition of their enterprise.

Hand-assembling a Dupont pen.

E.E. Ercolessi

E. ERCOLESSI ARE THE BEST-KNOWN pen retailers in Italy, with a tradition of marketing quality pens under their own trademark. The business was established in 1921 at Via Torino 48, Milan by Edgardo Ercolessi (the other "E" is for his wife Elvira), and later moved to a more prestigious address at Corso Vittorio Emanuele 15.

Edgardo Ercolessi saw great potential for the fountain pen in northern Italy. He began to insert advertisements for his shop in the *Corriere della Sera*, a leading newspaper, *Le Vie d'Italia* and in other Italian publications. When visiting the cinema, patrons were reminded of the shop with advertisements during the intervals. By the 1940s Milan's trams journeyed around the city emblazoned with advertisements for E.E. Ercolessi in a brilliant red lettering. These bore the strapline, *E.E. Ercolessi – Penne e Matite* (pens and pencils), stressing that they were a writing-instrument shop and not just another stationer.

COMPANY FACTS

EST. 1921

Milan, Italy

Not applicable

Two shops in Milan

$ ★ ★ ★

Edgardo Ercolessi used his contacts in the pen manufacturing industry to have a range of proprietary brands made for his shop. The first pen was a black hard rubber safety pen almost certainly made by Eugenio Verga of Columbus (see pp.74–77).

Edgardo's friendship with Armando Simoni (of Omas) led to Omas producing a range of pens sold under the E.E. Ercolessi trademark almost continuously between the 1920s and 1950s, interrupted only by the war. Omas, then as now, were one of the leading and best-quality marques in Italy. The wise choice of Omas pens ensured that E.E. Ercolessi pens enjoyed a reputation for quality and commanded widespread respect. The pens were made in a wide range of fashionable celluloids and the nibs were marked with the three "E's" of E.E. Ercolessi. Collectors may like to note that they are usually also stamped with the year of manufacture.

E.E. ERCOLESSI 75TH

E E ERCOLESSI 75TH

The prestigious Milanese pen shop E.E. Ercolessi celebrated their 75th anniversary in 1996 with this special pen. It was made in collaboration with Omas and recalls the friendship between Edgardo Ercolessi and Armando Simoni, founders of the respective houses. Over the years Omas has made many special pens for retail by Ercolessi, and this special commemorative pen has been made in Ercolessi's green signature color and is packaged with a bottle of green ink. The design is derived from the earliest Omas pens of the 1920s, but also has several similarities with the British Swan Visofil made in the mid 1930s and a favorite pen of E.E. Ercolessi's Paola Maggi.

The E.E. Ercolessi 18-ct. gold nib is a traditional design and does not follow the current fashion for two-color nibs.

*The first E.E. Ercolessi store opened at Via Torino
48, Milan in 1921. Today there are two stores, one in Corso
Vittorio Emanuele 15 and the other in Corso Magenta 25. They
are a mecca for Italian fountain-pen enthusiasts.*

Vintage E.E. Ercolessi pens were numbered in a sequential system; it is easy to identify the source of each pen as it coincides with the different manufacturers used; in addition to Columbus and Omas, these included, in rough chronological order, Kosca, Record, Minerva, Ancora, and Radius.

E.E. Ercolessi remains a family concern to this day and is run by Paola Maggi, who is well-known on the collecting circuit. E.E. Ercolessi celebrated their 75th anniversary in 1996, and to commemorate this milestone E E Ercolessi collaborated with Omas once again to produce a beautiful green and black celluloid pen.

COMPANY PRODUCTS

Retail pen shop known for
occasional commemorative pens

Faber-Castell

FABER-CASTELL IS MORE THAN 230 YEARS OLD. The company was founded in 1761, several decades before the French Revolution, and well before the U.S.A. became an independent nation. It is most probably the oldest manufacturing company in Germany that has remained in one family since its earliest days. The business is now an international group and one of the leading manufacturers of high-quality writing and drawing implements. The group is headed by Anton Wolfgang, Count von Faber-Castell. He is the sole managing partner of the company at the moment, and is the eighth generation of Fabers at the helm.

The business was originally founded by Caspar Faber, a Nuremberg cabinet maker, who married the daughter of a pencilmaker from Stein, near Nuremberg and started to make pencils in 1761. His son, Anton Wilhelm, gave the firm the name of A.W. Faber. The firm became truly successful when Lothar von Faber took over the factory in 1839. He introduced new production methods, standardized the product range, raised the quality, and began to mark each pencil with the A.W. Faber brand name. He was quite revolutionary and successfully petitioned the German Reichstag to create a trademark protection law which came into force in 1875. Lothar's younger brother Eberhard took over production of the American branch which had been set up in 1859. However, Eberhard and another brother, Johann, later separated from the main family business and went into business on their own account in America and Germany respectively.

COMPANY PRODUCTS

World's largest wooden pencil manufacturer, sales more than one billion pencils a year

Known for prestige designer writing instruments, ink, boxes, etc.

GRAF VON FABER-CASTELL COLLECTION

NIBS: six

GRAF VON FABER-CASTELL

Anton Wolfgang gave his name to this premium line as a guarantee of its quality. By 1996 the stable had expanded to include fountain pens and rollerballs, in addition to the existing ballpoint, mechanical pencil, and luxury traditional pencil.

Lothar Faber died in 1898 and the business passed to Count Alexander von Castell-Rüdenhausen who had married one of Lothar's granddaughters. The brand name was changed to A.W. Faber-Castell in order to express the quality of the product and also to differentiate the company from Johann Faber, whose business was eventually brought back into the family fold in 1928.

Faber-Castell's first pens were sold in 1908 and probably made by Kawecko. During the fountain pen boom of the 1920s Faber-Castell expanded their fountain-pen range in common with other German stationery manufacturers such as Pelikan. Their sales were not as strong as their competitors, however, and so Roland, Count von Faber-Castell decided to strengthen his position in the

COMPANY FACTS

EST. 1761

Stein, Nuremberg, Germany

Nine production sites worldwide

Worldwide

$ ★ ★

fountain-pen market by buying a pen manufacturer with a good reputation and he acquired a significant stockholding in Osmia, a former subsidiary of Parker, in 1935.

After the war Germany lost much of the export market which had benefited Faber-Castell. The familiar Osmia brand name was gradually replaced by that of Faber-Castell which was less well-known in the fountain-pen market. Production of fountain pens dwindled, finally ceasing in 1975 as Anton Wolfgang, Count von Faber-Castell restructured the business to concentrate on modern products for technical drawing and artist's use.

Twenty-one years later, in 1996, fountain pen production was revived to supplement the upmarket Graf von Faber-Castell line of writing instruments. At a time when there was a growing market in high-quality fountain pens they constituted a logical addition to a successful series of premium writing instruments. A rollerball was also introduced simultaneously to round off the product line. The combination of fine wood and silver is unique to Faber-Castell, and wood is a logical material for a pencil manufacturer to choose. The design is timeless because, rather than searching for a futuristic design or recreating an old version, it is based on the lines of a classic pencil.

It will be interesting to watch Faber-Castell's progress as they re-enter the fountain-pen market. Their commitment to quality, a strong brand name for prestige products, and a worldwide profile give them an advantage over many smaller companies.

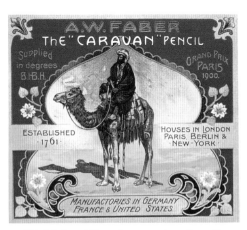

This label would have been on a box of pencils.

L. Michael Fultz - Penmaker

MIKE FULTZ WAS AMONG THE FIRST vintage fountain pen collectors to move into designing and manufacturing his own pens. He started penmaking as an adjunct to *Chicago Gold*, his business dealing in vintage fountain pens, vintage watches, and estate jewelry when he realized that there were no pens on the market comparable to the ornate filigrees of the Art Nouveau and Art Deco periods.

The pens combine the style and feel of vintage design with the reliability of a modern pen. Each has a precious metal casing over a pen by one of today's leading pen manufacturers. The majority of the L. Michael Fultz pens are made around a Parker International Duofold, chosen because they have a wide selection of nibs, a good ink flow, and are of a reasonable size and weight, but they are marketed under the L. Michael Fultz brand name and lifetime warranty. Each pen in the range is a limited edition, usually of 88 gold and 200 silver pens, but some smaller editions have also been issued.

The designs of each pen are original, and although Mike Fultz maintains one of the world's finest collections of vintage pens for reference, his pens should in no way be considered copies of older designs. The range includes work in the Art Deco, Art Nouveau, Art Moderne, Arts and Crafts, and Modern traditions. Were any criticism to be made of the Fultz pens, it would be that some designs rest uneasily on his preferred

COMPANY FACTS

 EST. late 1980s

 Chicago, U.S.A.

 Chicago. Some components made in Fultz workshop Milton, Wisconsin. Titanium pen produced in Escondido, California, U.S.A.

Best to order by post from Fahrney's Pens (U.S.A.). A growing network of agents worldwide includes Classic Pens (U.K.) and Exclusive Trading (Hong Kong). New designs are introduced in *Pen World International* magazine.

 $ ★ ★ ★ ★

pen, the Parker Duofold, however, and can appear somewhat squat. A preference for a thinner gauge of filigree, or a stream-lined shape to suit some of the more organic designs can easily be met as this is a company that delights in custom-design work.

Traditionally-skilled handcrafted work characterizes the Fultz pen from inception to the finished product. Typically a pen design will be sketched, then scaled to fit the specific pen. The company compounds its own gold and silver alloys; a rose gold and a silver compounded with nickel rather than copper to give a harder metal more resistant to tarnish. The design is transferred by hand to sheet metal and either hand-sawn for filigrees, or hand-hammered from both front and back for chased designs. The sheets are then rolled and soldered to size so that they fit the pen with the friction of precision with no need for glue, and the final details applied using either the lost-wax process or hand engraving. Because of Mike Fultz's desire to produce pens of the highest quality, 200 pens is typically a year's production for his jewelers and engravers.

Future plans for the company include more designs in the same vein, combining classic jewelry designs with modern writing. Because of his interest in the design and manufacture of jewelry Mike takes great pride in his custom designs and unique pens and is succeeding in his aim to make each design better than the last. His current project is to rejuvenate the "straight-holder" system of the 1890s, bringing up to modern writing standards and, in doing so, he aims to produce this pen wholly within his own workshops.

COMPANY PRODUCTS

Known for luxury market limited editions and custom orders.
Recent models include:

SNAKE
BUTTERFLY AND FLOWERS
TITANIUM PEN
MOORISH NIGHT
HOLY WATER SPRINKLER
BLUE LAGOON DESK SETS

At the time of writing most editions were still available

NIBS: wide range

SNAKE

BUTTERFLY AND FLOWERS

TITANIUM PEN

MOORISH NIGHT

SNAKE

An edition of 50 gold and 200 silver pens, introduced in 1993. The entwining coils of a snake were first wrapped around a pen by jewelers in the late 1890s and these early models are now coveted by many collectors. The Fultz snake has a greater depth to its filigree and uses sapphires for the eyes. This combination of precious metal and precious stones is a feature of many Fultz pens.

BUTTERFLY AND FLOWERS

An edition of 100 gold and 500 silver pens, introduced in 1994.

TITANIUM PEN

An edition of 100, introduced 1995. A simple design using one of the hardest metals yet developed.

MOORISH NIGHT

An edition of 88 gold and 200 silver pens, introduced in 1995. The delicate filigree and matching clip are now a sympathetic partner to the Parker Duofold body, and offer something that is a great improvement on the earlier Fultz pens, where the pocket clip was not designed in sympathy with the overlay.

Hakase

THE HAKASE ALL-HAND-MADE ORDER PEN is one of the world's most exclusive pens. The company was founded in China in 1932 and its full name, Mannenhitsu Hakase, means "Dr. Fountain Pen." In 1939 the manager Yoshio Yamamoto returned to his native Japan and continued to work in the pen manufacturing industry. After the war he moved to Tottori, a city on the western seaboard of Honshu, the main island of Japan.

Harumi Tanaka joined the company in 1952 and remains their master craftsman to this day. Hakase started to make custom-made pens for Japanese pen aficionados in the 1970s, initially using components from larger Japanese concerns such as Sailor. The Hakase All-Hand-Made-Order Pen was launched in the mid 1980s, and as the name implies it is completely handmade from start to finish by Tanaka, right down to the nib which is especially ground to the customer's specification. The name of the customer and year of manufacture are engraved on the barrel, and the actual date of completion is engraved on the barrel end.

The handmade pen has been made in a range of traditional materials including hard rubber and celluloid over the last two decades, and also in a wide variety of colors. Since 1987 the company has also used natural materials including buffalo horn and tortoiseshell for its pens. Each pen is distinguished by the twin-nib motif on the clip. At present there are more than 2,500 customers on the Hakase mailing list and there is usually a waiting time of several months for an All-Hand-Made Order Pen, but if you are impatient Hakase will welcome you to their factory and store (see pp.190–191).

COMPANY FACTS	
EST.	1932
🏢	Tottori, Japan
🏭	Tottori, Japan
🚚	From above (store address in directory of stores)
$	★ ★ ★ to ★ ★ ★ ★

HAKASE

Master craftsman Harumi Tanaka was born in 1937 and has been with Hakase since 1952. Here he is seen in action, turning parts on a lathe at his workbench.

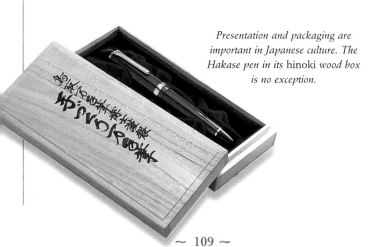

Presentation and packaging are important in Japanese culture. The Hakase pen in its hinoki wood box is no exception.

BARKENITE

Hakase's Barkenite is so-called because of the dark mahogany color and woodgrain appearance of the ebonite used to make the pen. No two pens ever have an identical pattern.

BLACK EBONITE

Black Ebonite is a traditional hard rubber made from latex "vulcanized" with sulfur. The Hakase Black Ebonite pen is polished to a soft black gloss.

TORTOISESHELL

Hakase's tortoiseshell pens were introduced in 1990 and 1991. The barrel is made from natural tortoiseshell using the cream marbling to best effect. As tortoiseshell is made from a living material it will expand and contract as temperatures and humidity change. To compensate for shrinkage and expansion parts are reinforced with ebonite.

CELLULOID

Hakase favor a palette of vibrant jade green, lapis blue, and rich brown celluloids, used either as single colors or with contrasting trim. Marbled and woodgrain colors are also popular, and both pencils and fountain pens are made.

COMPANY PRODUCTS

Known for handmade pens in a variety of traditional styles and materials including barkenite, ebonite, buffalo horn, tortoiseshell, and celluloid.

NIBS: ground to individual order

BLACK EBONITE

TORTOISESHELL

CELLULOID

Lamy

L AMY IS NO NEWCOMER to the world writing-instrument market. In fact the first fountain pens were made in Heidelberg as long ago as 1930. The company was founded by Joseph Lamy, who had worked as an export manager for Parker and had also helped them to set up business in Germany. He established the Orthos Fullhalterfabrik at the age of 32 with just one other employee, producing the Orthos pen and pencil in a style very similar to that of Parker.

C.J. Lamy purchased Artus in 1942 in order to obtain their injection-molding machines and produced an expanded range of Artus pens. He continued to acquire new patents and produced the Lamy 27 in 1952. This was the first pen to carry the Lamy name, 22 years after he had founded the company. It was a streamlined pen with a hooded nib, probably influenced by the Parker 51, and sold well in Germany thanks to Joseph Lamy's marketing skills.

Dr. Manfred Lamy, Joseph's son, joined the family firm in 1962. He orchestrated a

LAMY 2000

The Lamy 2000, designed by Gerd A. Muller, has been in production since 1966. It was a radical departure for Lamy and heralded the new direction which the company has followed during the last four decades. The range comprises fountain pen, ballpoint pen, four-color ballpoint, and pencil. It has only ever been offered in one size (large) and the now famous industrial finish of Makrolon reinforced by fiberglass and brush-finished stainless steel with a solid steel spring-operated clip.

LAMY LADY

complete change of direction for the business, bringing in Gerd A. Muller, an industrial designer and follower of the Bauhaus School. The first pen from this partnership was the Lamy 2000 introduced in 1966.

Modern functional design has been the characteristic of Lamy products ever since. The company claims to create a market demand with its products, rather than to follow market trends. The majority of Lamy's production is aimed at the school and youth market and it offers an enormous range of inexpensive writing instruments. Its top-range pens are aimed at people who appreciate contemporary design.

Some of today's most highly-regarded designers have been brought in from outside to work for Lamy. In addition to Gerd A. Muller, these have included Mario Bellini, Wolfgang Fabian, and Yang. Lamy have a string of design awards to their credit. Every single stage of development and production is carried out in-house using the most modern production methods. Some parts are partially handmade, and their top-range pens are hand-assembled.

LAMY LADY

The Lamy Lady is Lamy's first porcelain pen, developed in association with Rosenthal A.G. and launched in 1994. The two surface designs are by the Indonesian artist Yang (Sharon Jodjaja), while the shape was designed by Wolfgang Fabian, the designer of many successful Lamy pens. It has no clip, and two pips on the cap and barrel prevent it from rolling away. At present it is only available as a fountain pen.

LAMY PERSONA

The Lamy Persona was designed by Mario Bellini who is one of Italy's best-known industrial designers and architects. It was launched in 1990 and features a ribbed body, ripple ring grip and quill-like nib. Its innovative retractable clip is completely embedded in the cap and raised by thumb pressure. The range comprises fountain pen, ballpoint, and rollerball and is offered in platinum-plated, titanium-plated and black finishes.

COMPANY FACTS

Est. 1930

🏢 Heidelberg, Germany

🏭 Heidelberg, Germany

🚚 Worldwide

$ ★ ★

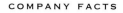

COMPANY PRODUCTS

Wide range of writing instruments

LADY
PERSONA
LAMY 2000

NIBS: six: extra-fine, fine, medium, broad, medium-oblique, broad-oblique

INKS: bottles and cartridges

LeBoeuf

L EBOEUF IS A COMPANY THAT has been brought back from the dead. The original company was founded in Springfield, Massachusetts around 1918 by Frank LeBoeuf, who had patented a process to make celluloid pens. The LeBoeuf pens of the 1920s came in a rainbow of unique colors and were advertised as unbreakable because they had a metal lining. The company was always in financial difficulties and sold parts worth more than $1 million, including mechanisms, to A.T. Cross in an attempt to discharge its debts, but was unable to stave off bankruptcy in 1933. Their pioneering celluloid pens are very rare today.

```
COMPANY FACTS

EST.   c.1918

🏢    Dallas, Texas, U.S.A.

🏭    Heidelberg, Germany

🚚    Worldwide

$     ★ ★
```

OPAL COLLECTION

The Gold and Silver Opal Collection comprises fountain pen, ballpoint, and rollerball and is available in either sterling silver or gold-plate. They come in a handcrafted cherry-wood box, the lid of which is a decorative porcelain tile.

COMPANY PRODUCTS

Known for high-quality pens

OPAL COLLECTION
LA PLUME COLLECTION
LE PRIX!
VARIOUS LIMITED EDITIONS

NIBS: range

In 1994 Geoffrey Dart bought the name and designed a new range of writing instruments. The new LeBoeuf began selling products in 1995. The pens are made from gold, silver, or lacquer over a brass core and have the signature Australian Opal in the cap crown. LeBoeuf also produce custom-made cherry-wood boxes which can incorporate the logo's corporate artwork.

The choice of famous golfer Greg Norman to endorse a limited-edition pen was an astute move. It created a brand awareness at a time when there was media interest in celebrity pen collectors, and landed LeBoeuf the cover of important trade magazines. LeBoeuf are launching a range of new models and are planning considerable worldwide expansion.

The Greg Norman Signature Pen, a limited edition of 3,086 pens endorsed by the champion golfer. LeBoeuf's best-known modern pen features a lacquer cap with facsimile signature, opal cap top, and a signed and numbered box.

LA PLUME COLLECTION

LE PRIX! COLLECTION

LA PLUME COLLECTION

The La Plume Collection comprises fountain pen, ballpoint, and rollerball and is available in either sterling silver or gold-plate, black or burgundy lacquer.

LE PRIX! COLLECTION

The Le Prix! Collection comprises fountain pen, ballpoint, and rollerball and is available in four lacquer colors; black, racing red, electric blue, and flash yellow.

Montblanc

MONTBLANC ARE THE BEST-KNOWN BRAND of quality pens in the world. Their extremely successful marketing slogan, "Montblanc—The Art of Writing" has given them worldwide recognition, and because they only make an upmarket product they are perceived as the ultimate upmarket brand.

The small business that was to become Montblanc was founded in Hamburg in 1908. An entrepreneur called Claus Johannes Voß had moved to the Hanseatic city after the opening of the free port in 1888. Voß had business experience around the world, and was looking for a new product with which to become involved. He was introduced to a technical engineer, August Eberstein and his partner Alfred Nehemias who were about to abandon their fledgling business in Berlin, which made the Rouge et Noir safety pen, through lack of capital. Voß and a banker, Max Koch, refinanced the company and took on the Hamburg Office Supply Firm as a sleeping partner.

The new company moved into premises in a multistory factory called the *Industriepalast*. A photograph taken soon after they opened shows the workforce as Eberstein, a foreman, 11 lathe operators and ten female assistants. The Simplo-Filler Pen Co., as the company was called, established agencies abroad and began to make eye-dropper-filling pens in the style of the day. Between 1909 and 1914 Koch, Nehemias, and Eberstein left the company through debt, death, and desertion respectively, leaving Voß to recruit the new partners who were to guide the company through the next decades.

COMPANY FACTS

EST. 1908

Hamburg, Germany

Hamburg, Germany

Worldwide

$ ★ ★ to ★ ★ ★ ★

The company developed an original safety pen with a metal pin in the cap which protected the nib when the pen was closed and enjoyed respectable sales. The Rouge et Noir name was changed at the outbreak of hostilities with France in 1914 to its nickname Rotkäppchen derived from the red cap top. Later a white cap top was chosen as being less conspicuous and a new

MONTBLANC
der elegante
Sicherheitsfüllhalter
für weisse Westen.

|57|

Montblanc was fast to recognize the value of strong
advertising. Here they promote their leak-free pens –
excellent for white waistcoats!

name had to be found for the pens. An apocryphal story has it
that Voß, playing cards with the well-known businessman Carl
Schalk, passed around the still unnamed pen, causing Mr Schalk
to suggest with a clever wink over his pince-nez: "Why not call
it 'Montblanc'? It is after all, like the mountain, black at the
bottom, white on top, and the greatest among its peers."

By 1910, the new name, Montblanc, had been given to all Simplo writing instruments. It was spelt as two words, Mont Blanc, with a mountain symbol between the two. In 1913 the white cap top (which could not be copyrighted) was modified to the white star "snowline" (which could be copyrighted) and has been used as the trademark ever since. It is now one of the best-known symbols for an elite international brand.

During World War I the firm Germanized its name to Simplo Füllfedergesellschaft and became completely self-sufficient in nib production, gold nibs having previously been imported from America and England. It developed strong patriotic sales in Germany and to the armed forces because overseas exports were no longer so easy.

During the 1920s and 1930s Simplo learned from America, the Parker Pen Co. in particular, and maintained a continuous and high-profile advertising campaign that far outstripped the efforts of their competitors. In addition to traditional store and media advertising, the Montblanc pen was advertised on airplanes, fleets of cars, and trade fairs.

MEISTERSTÜCK 149

The Montblanc Meisterstück 149 is the most famous writing instrument of our time. It is a statement as much as a pen and its distinctive white star can be seen peeping out of pockets throughout the world.

COMPANY PRODUCTS

Known for quality pens, stationery, and accessories

MEISTERSTÜCK
MEISTERSTÜCK TRAVELER
MEISTERSTÜCK GRAND COLLECTION
MEISTERSTÜCK SOLITAIRE
MONTBLANC CLASSIC
MONTBLANC NOBLESSE
LIMITED EDITIONS

NIBS: up to eight: extra-fine, fine, medium, oblique-medium, broad, oblique-broad, double broad, oblique double broad

INKS: bottles and cartridges

The company was reorganized and expanded by Ernst Rösler who had joined in 1919 and was to play an important role for many years to come. During the economic crisis of 1929–30 Rösler decided that his partners had not shown sufficient financial prudence and he had the company's articles of association rewritten, leaving him as the sole responsible party for business operations and decisions. He installed automatic machinery, established a toolworks, and increased the staff to around 500. The Montblanc trademark expanded to cover stationery folders, notebooks, pen and pencil cases, erasers, notepad boxes, photograph albums, writing paper, ink, and accessories, anticipating the product lines of today. Indeed the first specialty Montblanc stores had been opened in 1919 to provide direct sales support for these lines. Stationers Stoffhaas Brothers were taken on as partners for the first store in Hamburg and as the project grew in success a network of stores eventually covered Germany.

After Germany's surrender in 1945 Montblanc were no longer able to supply sufficient stock to their stores to make them economically viable. Added to this, customers expected to find a range of different brands in specialty shops and department stores. It is a tribute to the quality of the products that they were able to hold their own in this environment.

Montblanc had not suffered unduly during the war. They had been allowed to manufacture replacement parts for pens providing this did not interfere with the war effort. From time

Looking to possible future growth, Montblanc expanded their premises in 1989. Their origin was not forgotten, however, and the new entrance mirrored, detail for detail, that of Montblanc's original building.

to time a replacement part met up with other replacement parts in the factory and a complete pen was created. At the end of the war the existing stocks of parts enabled Montblanc production to be resumed swiftly.

By the mid 1950s Montblanc had developed their flagship 140 series Masterpiece range to what they regarded as perfection. The public agreed and they have remained in production ever since. The classic black Montblanc 149 is now a cultural icon and has outlasted changes to the remainder of the Montblanc stable caused by fashion or technology.

147 TRAVELER

MEISTERSTÜCK GRAND

The 147 Traveler is the
first Montblanc travel
fountain pen. It has a
cartridge holder that fills
from the top of the pen and
has room for a spare
cartridge. It is available in
black and burgundy.

MEISTERSTÜCK GRAND

The Meisterstück Grand
Collection are large,
but not as much as the
149. It comprises the 146
fountain pen, mechanical
pencil, ballpoint, rollerball,
and document marker.

MONT
BLANC

MEISTERSTÜCK SOLITAIRE

By 1976 Dr. Jürgen Rösler, who had succeeded his father at the helm of the firm, realized that Montblanc could only expand with a new plant and a massive capital injection. He also decided that there were no suitable successors in the founding families for management of the company. Accordingly he approached Alfred Dunhill, who had been trading with Montblanc for some time, seeing them as a suitable source of capital and also a compatible company. Both firms understood the importance of a highly-positioned brand image, high standards, and a discriminating target group of customers. Alfred Dunhill wanted to expand their writing-instrument division and needed suitable manufacturing facilities and in order to maintain their 40%–80% share of the luxury market, Montblanc needed to expand, and for this they needed Alfred Dunhill. The merger took place in 1977 with Dunhill acquiring a majority shareholding, and taking outright control in 1985.

MEISTERSTÜCK SOLITAIRE

The Meisterstück Solitaire is the ultimate Montblanc pen for the world's affluent. There are several versions in precious metals, each individually numbered:
- *.950 platinum with 18-ct. gold trim*
- *18-ct. white and yellow gold chevron*
- *vermeil*
- *sterling silver*
- *Solitaire Doué, with sterling-silver cap*

Most sizes of Masterpiece fountain pen are made as standard, with accompanying ballpoint, rollerball, and pencil.

*Montblanc entered the limited edition market
in 1992 with a series of limited edition pens dedicated to artists,
literary greats, and patrons of the arts. Some models proved wise
investment, the first of the series, the Lorenzo de' Medici, selling to
collectors for five times its original price in less than five years
after it was launched. So far the series has honored Lorenzo de'
Medici, Octavian (the Roman Emperor Augustus), René Lalique,
Ernest Hemingway, Louis XIV, Voltaire, The Prince Regent (King
George IV of England), Agatha Christie, and others.*

The Montblanc brand name remained distinct and continued
on an upward trend throughout the 1980s and 1990s, helped by
a slick marketing campaign, the expansion of its associated
products, and the opening of a network of Montblanc Boutiques
throughout the world—a strategy that would have been
familiar to the far-sighted Ernst Rösler during the interwar years.
Montblanc is now part of the Vendôme group of luxury
companies alongside Cartier, Alfred Dunhill, Karl Lagerfeld, and
other names well-known in upmarket homes and looks set to
retain its position as the world's best-known luxury pen well
into the twenty-first century.

Hervé Obligi

SOME OF TODAY'S MOST STRIKING and unique pens are made by Hervé Obligi, a French *sculpteur—pierre dures*, or artist-craftsman in stone. The art of stone inlay reached a pinnacle in Italy during the seventeenth and eighteenth centuries, when panels and furniture were inlaid with stone specimens. In the late eighteenth and nineteenth centuries pictures and micro-mosaics recreated the craftsmanship of Ancient Rome and served as souvenirs of the Grand Tour.

During the late nineteenth century French artisans redis-covered the charms of working in stone; Fabergé often used it for decorative objects, and Cartier produced a rich collection of luxury stone goods. Hervé Obligi learned the skilled techniques and processes of the lapidary's art as a restorer of applied arts, working notably for Cartier, in particular on their clocks.

A desire to create, rather than endlessly repair, led him to set up his own workshop where he undertakes commissions for tables, sculptures, and jewelry. His clients include institutions, connoisseurs, and collectors. He works in "hard" stones and minerals from around the world including coral, agate, jade, lapis lazuli, chalcedony, jasper, quartz, rock crystal, gold, and silver.

COMPANY FACTS

EST. 1984

93100 Montreuil-sous-bois, France

as above

From the workshop, as above
tel: 33 (1) 48 57 17 54
fax: 33 (1) 48 70 94 07

$ ★ ★ ★ ★

He was asked to make his first pen by a friend in 1992. A master stoneworker had not made a pen before because of inherent problems with the material; it is cumbersome, fragile, and not easily turned into the cylindrical tube needed for a pen. A pen takes two to three months to make depending on the type and model. Hervé Obligi designs his own models, but also takes into account customers' suggestions as to form, color, and the type of pen base. Each pen is entirely handmade in his workshop (apart from the proprietary pen base), designed to match the contours of the hand, and write comfortably without being too heavy.

LE STYLO ABEILLE

STYLO ARGENT

LE STYLO ABEILLE

The Stylo Abeille, or "bee pen", is regarded by Hervé Obligi as his most important pen because it combines all the techniques involved in working with hard stones: lathe work, inlay work, marquetry, and engraving. It is contoured to match the hand and made of tiger's eye, bassanite, coral, and gold. The base of the pen is a Sheaffer.

STYLO ARGENT

The Stylo Argent is made from Mexican agate, *oeil de faucon,* and solid silver. The base pen is a Waterman.

The Stylo Agate Mousse is made from moss-agate, onyx, purpurine, and gold. The base pen is a Waterman.

COMPANY PRODUCTS

Known for luxury handmade stone pens

NIBS: depends on base pen

Parker

George S. Parker.

Parker MUST RUN A CLOSE SECOND to Montblanc in the luxury pen market, and probably beats all comers hands down when it comes to selling writing instruments. They have a long and distinguished history stretching back over 100 years, making them the second-oldest pen company in the world, and their pens have been used by many famous figures from JFK to the British Royal family.

In the 1880s George S. Parker, a young teacher at the Valentine School of Telegraphy, Janesville, Wisconsin, U.S.A. obtained an agency of the John Holland Fountain Pen, and sold pens to his students in order to supplement his income. In common with most other pens of the time they had an erratic ink flow. The root of the problem appeared to be the pen's "feed". Parker set about improving this, and was successful. Encouraged by this improvement to the pen and the award of a patent on his invention on December 10, 1889, George S. Parker started to assemble and sell his own pens. The Parker Pen Company was born when an insurance salesman, W.F. Palmer, bought a half-interest in the business for $1,000.

Parker never looked back after the patent of the famous "Lucky-Curve" feed on December 4, 1894, a revolutionary yet simple feed designed with a curved rear. It ensured that when a pen was carried upright in a jacket pocket the nib would never flood as ink always drained back into the reservoir by capillary action from the curved end. It established Parker as the "clean" pen. Clean writing, clean fingers, and clean, ink-free pockets are all taken for granted today, but in the 1890s they represented an important step forward.

The Art Nouveau movement influenced the designers of the Parker Pen Company who created some of the most beautiful pens ever made with intricate overlays and filigrees of precious metals and mother-of-pearl. Some of these pens were produced in very small numbers and it is hardly surprising that such pens are extremely rare today.

*Poster from 1903, advertising the Parker Lucky
Curve Fountain Pen.*

Parker entered the 1920s with a new top-of-the-range pen
called the Duofold. It became an instant classic, and continues
to influence manufacturers and designers throughout the world
to this day. It employed all the design improvements from the
beginning of the century. The new pen led the whole industry

throughout the 1920s, a period which was the golden age of the fountain pen. It was larger, more colorful, and sold for $7, which was more than double the price of the average pen. Kenneth Parker (George's son), led the famous sales and advertising campaign which launched it in 1921.

The introduction of plastics in 1926 enabled new colors to be introduced in addition to the existing black or red pens. Parker's advertising stunts continued to keep these new pens in the public eye as they were dropped from the Empire State building or hurled into the Grand Canyon to demonstrate that they were unbreakable. The company opened many overseas factories at this time and today "Big Red" is almost synonymous with vintage fountain pen and the six sizes of Duofold, whose design was refined nearly every year, are the backbone of many collections of vintage pens.

During the Depression years, Parker bought a patent for a new filling mechanism from Professor Dahlberg at the University of Wisconsin, then invested $125,000 developing it over the next five years. The system would be used until 1948, initially on a radical new pen known as the "Vacuum-Filler." The pen was advertised as holding 102% more ink than previous pens, and the amount of ink remaining could be seen through the transparent windows of the barrel which was made of a unique

Parker became very innovative with color once new plastics were available.

SNAKE PEN

*The legendary Snake pen, one of the extremely
rare designs influenced by the Art Nouveau
movement. One of these pens was auctioned at
Bonhams, London in 1993 and fetched a world-
record $22,000.*

"BIG RED"

*The Lucky Curve Duofold, launched in 1921,
was nicknamed the "Big Red" by collectors and
was a pen that changed the direction of the
American fountain pen industry forever. It
remains the standard by which the success of all
vintage and many modern pens are judged.*

PARKER 51

*The Parker 51 is arguably the best pen ever
made. It was the first fully reliable pen that
wrote first time, did not leak, and whose ink
dried quickly. Millions are still in everyday use,
and its design was enormously influential.*

PARKER 75

*.The Parker 75 was another long-standing
favorite among Parker users. Produced through
four decades it has been available in a wide
range of finishes. The success of Parker 75
limited editions probably inspired other
companies to produce their own limited editions.
This example was made using brass salvaged
from the HMS Queen Elizabeth, sunk in Hong
Kong harbor.*

"BIG RED"

PARKER 51

PARKER 75

laminated plastic. Another feature of the Vacumatic was the two-color nib, engraved with the new arrow trademark, which was also on the new pocket-clip designed by Joseph Platt, a famous New York artist. The Vacumatic was every bit as revolutionary as the advertising claimed, it eliminated 14 parts used in older pens, and was an instant success when launched nationwide on March 18, 1933. The best tribute to the Vacumatic comes from Parker's competitors including Sheaffer, Waterman, Conklin, and Wahl-Eversharp, who all launched their own laminated plastic pens with a visible ink supply during the 1930s.

The Parker 51 enjoys a reputation among collectors as the best pen ever made, supported by worldwide sales in excess of $400 million. Development was completed in 1939, Parker's 51st anniversary, hence the unusual name. The 51 was so different to previous pens that Parker advertised it as being "like a pen from another planet." The streamlined, rocket-shaped pen used Parker's new quick-drying ink (Quink) which "writes dry with wet ink," had a new smooth-writing tubular nib, and always wrote first time. Pens made in 1941, the first year of production, are identified by an aluminum stud each end of the pen, replaced by pearl-gray studs the following year. The pen underwent slight modification in 1947–48 with the introduction of the Aerometric filling system which used a transparent Pliglass ink-reservoir.

Numerous versions of the 51 were produced between 1939 and 1972. Many of these are quite common and still in use today. Rare models of the 51 include the Empire State with a

COMPANY FACTS

EST. 1889

Newhaven, England

Main factory in Newhaven, England

Worldwide

$ ★ ★ to ★ ★ ★ ★

yellow and green gold cap, the solid-gold Presidential, the rolled-silver model, and some of the early colors especially mustard-yellow, Nassau green, and cedar blue.

During the 1940s demand exceeded production, and the 51 was such a prestigious pen that U.S. servicemen were able to use them as currency in war-torn Europe, along with nylons and chocolate.

Special edition cap band and two-tone nib of the Vacumatic pen.

VACUMATIC

The Vacumatic was made in a number of rare variations, including a Holy Water Sprinkler, a Doctor's set which included a thermometer case, and the luxurious range of Imperial Vacumatics with gold-plated or solid gold caps.

DUOFOLD MANDARIN

FRONTIER

RIALTO

SONNET

MANDARIN

The Mandarin Duofold, limited to 10,000 pens, heralded the re-styled Duofold which was first offered in 1996. It is based on the famous Mandarin Yellow Lucky Curve of the late 1920s.

FRONTIER

Parker's current "budget" pen, available in a range of colors and finishes.

RIALTO

Parker's pen for the young and trendy.

SONNET

Parker's latest pen, and their first all-new design for some time. It is selling extremely well and is available in a wide range of finishes and price ranges. Its soft nib is a new development for Parker.

Quink ink also played an important role in the success of Parker pens of this time as it contained Solv-X, a solvent specifically designed to clean the materials used to make Parker components, and enabled Parker to become synonymous with reliability.

The approach of the Parker Pen Company to the difficult postwar years was to innovate, producing the tungsten ball and their first ink cartridge. These advances have had such a longlasting impact on the Parker range that today we take them for granted.

The T-Ball Jotter was launched in 1954 and is still going strong. The tungsten (hence "T"-Ball) was the first ball specifically designed for writing. Previous pens had used a common steel ballbearing and had neither the same reputation for reliability, nor smooth writing.

The modern convenience of the ink-cartridge was introduced in 1960 with the Parker 45, reputedly named because it was as easy to load as a Colt .45 revolver. It was now possible to carry refills around in your pocket, rather than search for a bottle of ink, and in an emergency the unique flick-tip provided a hidden ink reserve. To follow this success Parker was awarded the Royal warrant as sole supplier of pens and inks to the British Royal Household in 1962, an honor which it retains to this day.

The Parker 75 is a true design classic. It was introduced in 1964 and featured the new contoured grip with adjustable nib that could be turned to suit an individual's style of writing. This stylish new pen was a delight to write with, production spanned four decades, and it sold literally throughout the world. Several popular limited-edition 75 pens were made in the 1960s and 1970s, anticipating the current fashion for limited-edition products by two decades. By the time the 75 was discontinued in 1993 it had been made in a wide variety of finishes from 18-ct. gold to lunar material recovered by Apollo 15.

The Parker 75 succeeded the 51 as the preferred pen of statesmen, and Parker often custom-made 75s for use in historic events. In 1991 unique silver and 22-ct. gold-plated 75s crowned with sapphires were made for the signing of the Strategic Arms Reduction Treaty (START). Each pen is slightly different: Mikhail Gorbachev's pen was set with a red star sapphire while George Bush's has a blue star sapphire.

In 1970 Parker launched a futuristic pen made almost completely of titanium called the T-1. This pen truly had the look of the "Space Age," with its rocket-like styling and sleek, integral nib-unit. A small screw could adjust the nib width to reflect the writer's desired writing style. Titanium is one of the toughest metals known to man and it was soon discontinued, reputedly because of technical problems. The futuristic pen was succeeded by the Model 50 Falcon offered with a choice of nib grades instead of an adjustable nib. The pen was advertised as the first pen since the quill without a separate nib.

Parker has an uncanny knack for increasing sales in uncertain times. Turnover increased by nearly fifty percent during the late 1980s despite a world recession. This was due to the U.K. management team's successful buy-out of the Writing Instrument Division in February 1986 and their decision to relaunch the most famous Parker pen, the Duofold, under its new name, the Duofold Centennial. (The pen's name celebrated the approaching centenary of the company.) It reflected the new management's ethos of developing and promoting their top brands and allowing the benefits to spread throughout the company.

The charm of the Duofold lies in the combination of traditional style, craftsmanship, and quality with state-of-the-art technology. It appealed to people who wanted to replace their existing pen as well as many new customers who had probably never considered buying a premium pen before. The memorable television commercial featuring a Rolls Royce boosted sales of a pen that was competitively priced, yet, more importantly, suited everybody's handwriting by offering an unbeatable range of 24 different nib grades.

COMPANY PRODUCTS

Known for writing instruments for all market segments, ink, and accessories

DUOFOLD
FRONTIER
RIALTO
SONNET
45
VARIOUS LIMITED EDITIONS

NIBS: between 11 and 24 depending on model

INKS: wide range of bottles and cartridges:
Quink, the standard range, introduced 1933
Penman, a slightly thicker ink with more intense colors, launched 1994

Parker is now part of the Gillette stationery group with Waterman, Papermate, and Liquid Paper. The product lines have been given new names, rather than numbers, to make them more customer-friendly and the first range of entirely new pens—the Sonnet—has been launched. The new management are hard at work designing new top-of-the-range products expecting that the benefits will trickle down through their range.

The Sonnet line is available in up to 18 finishes,
and comprises fountain pen, rollerball, ballpoint,
and pencil.

Platinum

PLATINUM ARE ONE OF Japan's leading quality pen manufacturers with a long history compared to many of their
competitors. Although founded in 1919 they were not one of
that country's first companies to make fountain pens, rather one
of the most long-lived. Platinum's roots can be traced to one of
Japan's many businesses importing Western fountain pens in the
early part of this century when Syunichi Nakata opened a store
in Okayama. In 1924 he moved to Tokyo and founded a
manufacturing concern, Nakaya Seisakusho, which was later
renamed Platinum after the precious metal. There have been
two further name changes since then, but on each occasion the
brand Platinum has been retained.

Platinum's initial success came from selling pens mail-order
to remote parts of Japan and overseas exports. They also made
proprietary brands for Tokyo department stores. Platinum
launched their own lines of *Maki-e* lacquer pens in the 1930s in
order to compete with Namiki. The war brought an inevitable
halt to production and Nakata was seconded to a munitions
factory which made the Zero fighter. After the war he resumed
production and launched the first ballpoint pen in Japan in 1948.
The next generation of the family to run the business, Tosaburo
Nakata, developed a rollerball known as the Autopen in 1966
which by 1980 had sold more than one billion units.

During the 1960s and 1970s Platinum introduced a number
of new pens including the "Platinum-Platinum" range of metal
pens and, in keeping with the spirit of the times, a range of
leather pens called the Amazonas. They were covered in either

---

COMPANY PRODUCTS

Quality fountain pens in a variety of styles including

MAKI-E LACQUER
ZOGAN
VARIOUS LIMITED EDITIONS

NIBS: range

INKS: range

PLATINUM 70TH

A series of limited-edition pens was released in September 1988 to celebrate Platinum's 70th year. Each was a numbered edition of 1,000 pens. There was a range of colors and materials, each distinguished by its decorative cap band. This example is made from traditional ebonite.

ZOGAN

Zogan is a type of metal engraving and inlay. This model is produced in the Higo area of Kumamoto on Japan's most westerly main island, which is a traditional focus for Zogan production. The cap band is decorated with gold inlay in a variety of different traditional motifs, including cherry blossom, arabesque, and streamline (shown here).

PLATINUM 70TH

ZOGAN

MAKI-E

PLATINUM 80TH

MAKI-E

Maki-e *Raden is one of the most decorative styles of* Maki-e *techniques, using layers of cut shells such as nacre, pearl or abalone. This* Maki-e *model was introduced in April 1996 and is produced in the Kaga area of Ishikawa in the center of Japan which is famous for its* Maki-e *production. The triangular scale of the* Rinmon *is based on the old textile design of Kimono costume used in traditional* Noh *drama performances.*

PLATINUM 80TH

To celebrate their 80th anniversary, Platinum recreated some of their vintage designs, which went on sale as limited editions in July 1996. The original gold filigree Kinbari Sukashi Mannenhitu *was made in 1925. This reproduction limited edition is available in two versions, gold or silver over ebonite, and the filigree is engraved with an elaborate arabesque pattern.*

COMPANY FACTS

EST. 1919

Tottori-shi, Japan

Various locations in Japan

Mainly Far East

$ ★ ★ to ★ ★ ★ ★

snake, lizard, shark, crocodile, or Surinam toad-skin. In today's politically correct world these are now highly collectable as curios. Their longest-lasting model from this time was the 3776 series designed by the novelist Haru Umeda, who was himself a pen collector. The name 3776 was chosen because it is the height in meters of Mt. Fuji, the volcano which dominates Honshu, the main island of Japan, and holds a compelling fascination for her people. The pen was first introduced in 1978 and with a few minor restylings along the way is still in production today in a greatly expanded range of finishes. Not every pen is as expensive as their luxurious top-of-the-range *Maki-e* models, each of which must be considered as an individual work of art in its own right, and retails at around $6,000.

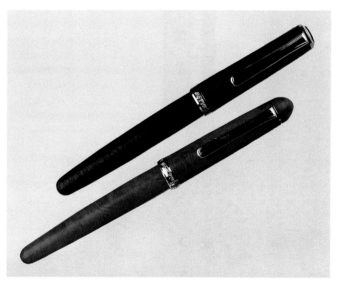

The changing shape of the 3776. The sandblasted briar is made to the 1980s pattern, while the light briar is the streamlined profile adopted in the 1990s.

Recife

RECIFE IS A YOUNG FRENCH COMPANY. It was founded in 1987 by Leo Smaga and Stephen Arnal who were both born in 1963 and met in a French business school after studying art. In 1988 Stephen designed a collection in vivid colors seeing the pen as a fashion accessory and their first break came when the British retail fashion chain Next placed an order. Their current clients include Brummel and the Conran Shop.

Recife pens are all designed in-house to keep the same spirit in every model. The firm believes that small is beautiful, employing only 17 people in their workshop. Eighty percent of production is exported and there is a collectors' club in the United States. Prices are kept low—usually under $80 and the target market is the young and trendy crowd, women, and collectors.

Recife believe that the look of their pens is an important part of their appeal. This is based around their striking and exclusive materials; marbled resins, mystique, and colored ebonite (hard rubber). They are currently the only manufacturer to use rippled hard rubber which was last popular in the 1920s before the use of celluloid permitted a wider range of colors to be made. Recife's manufacturing process depends on the materials being worked. The mystique and ebonite pens are handmade, while machines are used for resin, plexiglass, and metal.

COMPANY FACTS	
EST.	1987
🏢	Meudon la Forêt, Cedex, France
🏭	Meudon la Forêt, Cedex, France
🚚	100 stockists worldwide, not necessarily pen stores
$	★ ★

Ebonite is made from latex, a sustainable resource harvested from the rubber tree by rubber tappers in tropical forests. The natural latex is heated, rippled, or colored with pigments and vulcanized with 32% sulfur before being formed into rods. The cured rods are hand-turned to make pen components. Recife view the return to ebonite as a positive step for the environment, and are donating a portion of the proceeds from the sale of their ebonite pens in the United States to a rainforest charity.

PRESS COLLECTION—MASTER ROLLER

ANDY WARHOL MONA LISA

MYSTIQUE

LE VIRAGO

MASTER ROLLER

The Press Collection Master Roller. Recife place as much emphasis on style as on function, and give equal importance to the rollerball and ballpoint as they do the fountain pen— providing it looks good!

ANDY WARHOL MONA LISA

The Recife Andy Warhol pens are limited editions from their flagship Mystique range and are produced under license from the Andy Warhol Foundation. Made from Recife's "mystique" material, each pen is unique as the colors never combine the same way twice. The silver-plated band is engraved with Andy Warhol's signature and the trim is inspired by Warhol's first 1960s foil-decorated factory. The Mona Lisa comes in a numbered edition of 5,000 fountain pens and 5,000 rollerball points in colors matching Warhol's 1978 Mona Lisa *silkscreen.*

MYSTIQUE

The Mystique offers vibrant color lines in striking color combinations. The material is exclusive to Recife and is derived from the study of an old English craft. It took more than two years of intensive testing and research to develop. There are two models, Victory and Replica, each available in fountain pen, rollerball, and ballpoint. Solid gold nibs are available.

LE VIRAGO

Virago is Recife's most recent pen and offers an uncommon look and texture. It is available in fountain pen, ballpoint, and rollerball.

The Andy Warhol Marilyn Monroe is companion to the
Mona Lisa and comes in a number edition of 7,500
fountain pens and 7,500 rollerballs, in colors matching one
of Warhol's famous 1967 screenprints of Marilyn Monroe.

COMPANY PRODUCTS

Known for inexpensive pens for fashion
conscious, and collectors

PRESS COLLECTION
ANDY WARHOL
MYSTIQUE
LE VIRAGO

NIBS: usually gold-plated

INKS: bottles and vials

Rotring

ROTRING ARE WORLD-FAMOUS for their superior technical drawing pens, and their hi-tech approach is now being applied to a range of fountain pens. The company was founded in Hamburg by Wilhelm Riepe who established Tiku GmbH in 1928 to make inexpensive stylographic pens similar to those he had seen in America, and which had first been developed by A.T. Cross in the 1870s (see pp. 85–90). The brand name "Tiku" was a corruption of Tinten-Kuli, from the German for ink and "Coolie" from a Chinese worker. Like the A.T. Cross Stylograph in America, the Tiku was popular as it was easy to use when carbon copies were needed. It was also cheaper to make than a conventional fountain pen which used an expensive precious metal—gold—for its nib. The company prospered, built a second factory, and enjoyed an enormous success on the export market. Wilhelm Riepe was exporting his Tiku to 34 countries within five years of its launch.

In 1945 Wilhem Riepe died and his son Helmuth inherited the business. He had to rebuild the business as well as the factory which had been destroyed during the war. He found a ready market in the occupying forces, and was soon supplying the Royal Air Force with 1,000 stylographs a month. New products were developed during the late 1940s and early 50s, and one of these, the Rapidograph was a technical drawing instrument which could be used to write quickly, and was partly developed and launched in the enormous American market. Today Rotring enjoys more than 60% of the world technical drawing instrument market.

In 1965 the company changed its name, to Rotring Werke Riepe K.G. *Roter Ring* in German means red ring, and this had been a distinctive feature of the firm's pens since the first Tiku. Rotring continued to expand throughout the 1970s, most importantly acquiring the American distribution company Koh-I-

COMPANY FACTS	
EST.	1928
🏢	Hamburg, Germany
🏭	Headquarters' factory, Hamburg, Germany
🚚	Worldwide
$	★

Noor in association with Pelikan A.G. Koh-I-Noor became a wholly owned subsidiary of Rotring after they acquired Pelikan's share in 1983, and is now important in the United States.

Rotring moved into the graphic and hobby market with its calligraphic fountain pen, the ArtPen, in 1984. The writing instrument division has continued to diversify and is no longer limited to the production of purely technical drawing instruments. A range of hi-tech metal pens is now produced, usually designed in-house.

COMPANY PRODUCTS

Known for technical drawing instruments and fountain pens

ESPRIT
600
700
RIVE/RIVETTE
LIMITED EDITIONS
ARTPEN

NIBS: varies between pens from one to 19 mainly calligraphic, italic, drawing nibs

INKS: bottles, cartridges, and drawing inks

ESPRIT

The Rotring Esprit is a light pen with a contoured grip. The collection is available as fountain pen, rollerball, ballpoint, pencil, or duo-pen (combining both pencil and ballpoint). All are made of anodized aluminum and finishes include matt silver, graphite, nautical blue, and tourmaline green. There are six widths of steel nib: extra-fine, fine, medium, medium-oblique, broad, and broad-oblique.

600

ARTPEN

600

The Rotring 600 series has a hexagonal body and diamond-cut grip. There is an adjustable code ring on the end of each model to show either the nib grade, or refill color in use. The collection comprises fountain pen, rollerball, ballpoint, mechanical pencil, and trio-pen (combining two colors of ballpoint and a mechanical pencil). All are made of brass with chrome finish in matt black or silver. The 600 Gold has an 18-ct. gold nib and the 600 Standard has a steel nib each with a choice of eight nib widths.

ARTPEN

The shape of the Rotring ArtPen comes from the quill and the dip pen, combining their balance with modern technology and a modern textured grip. It is made from matt black acrylic resin and has a vast range of hand-polished steel calligraphic nibs. There is a smaller range of nibs for white ink, as well as several sets.

Sheaffer

SHEAFFER IS ONE OF THE OLDEST existing pen companies, formed in 1912 by Walter A. Sheaffer. His friends cautioned him against investing his hard-earned life's savings in such an unpredictable business as fountain-pen manufacture.

Walter A. Sheaffer (1867–1946) was one of five children of Jacob Royer Sheaffer and Anna Eliza Wilton. Jacob ran a jewelry store in Bloomfield, Iowa but

Walter A. Sheaffer (1867–1946), founder of the company and its guiding light.

family financial circumstances forced Walter to leave high school and look for work before he had completed his education. Walter learned the fundamentals of the jewelry trade in Centerville and Unionville, before becoming a partner in his father's business in 1888. Sheaffer showed an astute business mind from the outset, selling his house to purchase first an eight-acre property and then a run-down 188-acre farm. By 1906 the farm was back in

shape and Walter traded it for a jewelry store in Fort Madison, Iowa. The deal also included $12,552 in store stock.

Walter A. Sheaffer had sold fountain pens both in his father's store and then in his own. At that time pens were usually filled from a bottle using an eye-dropper, which could be messy. There was a "self-filling" pen on the market, the Conklin crescent filler (see p.28), but this had an ungainly bulge on the side of the pen. Sheaffer developed a pen with a filling system that was to remain an industry standard until the 1960s. He eliminated the need for a messy eye-dropper by using a rubber sac such as Conklin's, and eliminated the bulge by developing a pivoted lever and pressure bar to deflate the sac. The lever fitted smoothly into a recess on the side of the pen barrel. He was granted a patent on August 25, 1908 to cover the new idea, but it was somewhat overshadowed by Henry Ford's introduction of the Model-T automobile the same year.

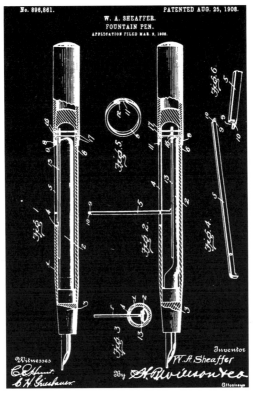

W.A. Sheaffer's original patent for a lever self-filling fountain pen, granted while he was still selling jewelry, some five years before the W.A. Sheaffer Pen Co. was incorporated.

COMPANY PRODUCTS

Known for a full range of pens for all prices, including Masterpiece and Luxury collections

TARGA MOIRÉ
CREST
LEGACY
NOSTALGIA
VARIOUS LIMITED EDITIONS

NIBS: six: extra fine, fine, medium, broad, stub, oblique

INKS: wide range of bottles and cartridges

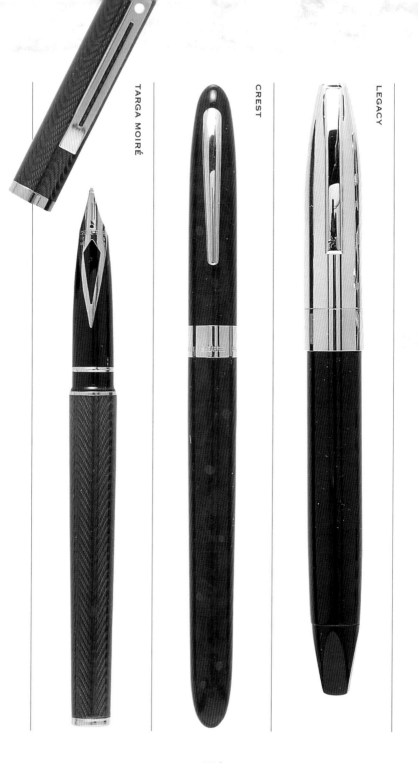

TARGA MOIRÉ

CREST

LEGACY

TARGA MOIRÉ

The well-known Targa range was launched in 1976, and more than 20 years later is as popular as ever. A range in Chinese lacquer is the latest addition to the collection and is available as a fountain pen and ballpoint in three iridescent colors: green, amber, and blue. Targa by Sheaffer is also made in various lacquer and metal finishes as well as silver and solid gold.

CREST

The Crest has been popular for a number of years now, and the range has expanded over time to offer a number of finishes. The collection includes fountain pen, rollerball, and ballpoint, offered in sterling silver, gold-plate, palladium electroplate, black lacquer, as well as the two newcomers Opalite Marine Green and Opalite Golden Brown.

LEGACY

The Sheaffer Legacy is a revival of the bold styling of the PFM (Pen For Men) of the 1960s, using a touchdown filling system. The collection comprises fountain pen, rollerball, and ballpoint and at present it is available in black with a choice of caps; black, palladium electroplate, and brushed gold electroplate.

NOSTALGIA

The Sheaffer Nostalgia is one of the best-looking recreations of a 1920s filigree pen made today. It is available with a matching ballpoint, and the range of accessories includes rocker blotter, letter knife, and crystal and silver inkwell, each with a sterling-silver foliate filigree design.

Original poster from 1951 advertising the
touchdown pen-filling device.

The pen with a revolutionary new filling mechanism was tried out on friends, and refined. Sheaffer's retail experience told him that it would be a success and a revised patent was granted in 1912. He entered the highly competitive arena of pen manufacture in 1912, aged 45 and in competition with 58 other companies in America. The jewelry store workshop became a factory with a staff of seven including Sheaffer's son Craig. Two salesmen, George Kraker and Ben Coulson, who had worked for Conklin, were taken on. The W.A. Sheaffer Pen Co. was officially incorporated on January 1, 1913. In the first year the company captured 3% of the writing-instrument market and chalked up sales of $100,000. Profits were $17,500 or 50% of the initial $35,000 invested by Sheaffer, Kraker, and Coulson.

COMPANY FACTS

Est. 1912–1913

Fort Madison, Iowa, U.S.A.

Main plant Fort Madison, satellites worldwide

Worldwide

$ ★ to ★ ★ ★ ★

The years from 1913 to the end of the 1920s were important to Sheaffer. They fought off larger companies who infringed their patents, moved to a larger factory, and started to make their own gold nibs. This was an important step forward as prior to 1917 all Sheaffer nibs had been shipped in from the East. Whenever the train was late, or a shipment did not arrive on time, production was seriously affected or halted entirely. In the early 1920s Sheaffer pens became a best-seller in America with the introduction of a lifetime nib (guaranteed for the life of the owner) and of colored radite (celluloid) pens. By 1925 Sheaffer accounted for 25% of all pen sales in America.

Sheaffer streamlined the shape of their pens during the 1930s and developed the Feathertouch two-way nib, a plunger filling system, and a visible ink supply. The company weathered the Depression and even introduced a profit-sharing scheme for staff. During the war Sheaffer expanded its factories and made products for the war effort including an automatic radio-tuning device for the armed forces. When civilian production restarted prices were kept at pre-war levels which encouraged sales. Four important introductions during the 1940s were the tubular Triumph nib, the spring clip, the first Sheaffer ballpoint pen of 1947, and the "touchdown" filling device which empties, cleans, and refills the pen in a single downstroke of the plunger.

The 1950s were a decade of great success for Sheaffer. A new factory was built after the old Morrison Plow Works, home to Sheaffer since 1916, was destroyed by fire. The 50 millionth Sheaffer pen was made in November 1951. The snorkel filling system was introduced in 1952, and was a "clean" system as a tube (or "snorkel") extended from the pen during filling, eliminating the need to submerge the nib in ink. It was promoted with transparent demonstration pens and greatly benefited the company's sales. In 1959 one of Sheaffer's most famous lines, the PFM (Pen For Men) was introduced designed specifically for a man's firm hand.

In 1966 Sheaffer became part of Textron Inc., a textile manufacturer, merging with another division the Eaton Paper Co. in 1976. The Targa range, introduced the same year, has been one of Sheaffer's most enduring products and is still in production. It typifies Sheaffer's approach to their pens, managing to be both conservative and innovative at the same time, and has been available in a wide range of colors and sold across all price ranges. It remains one of Sheaffer's most important models.

Sheaffer continue to place importance on customer service and sales and have a flourishing custom division. The Legacy, Targa, and Fashion ranges can be ordered in custom colors (minimum 500 units) and the Triumph Imperial can be made in custom colors for larger companies, with a minimum order of 10,000 units. In recent years Sheaffer have made exclusive pens for the London department store Harrods and for Classic Pens Ltd (see pp.78–81). The popularity of Sheaffer is such that when these appear for sale at Bonhams today they often sell for multiples of their original retail price.

The W.A. Sheaffer pen, Sheaffer's first limited edition, celebrating Walter Sheaffer's famous first pen patent. The pens also feature the early Sheaffer ball clip and are probably the only lever-filling fountain pens on the retail market.

Stipula

STIPULA SEEM TO HAVE PLUNDERED every civilization from Classical Greece onward in order to derive inspiration for their pens, and rather than produce a complete mangling of the Western heritage, has managed to produce a product that looks and feels right—yet remains quintessentially Italian. It may be one of Italy's youngest pen manufacturers, but in the last five years Stipula has managed to establish a varied stable of pens with many novel features.

The business started in Florence in 1973, primarily making trinketry for prestigious leather goods and became well-known for its lacquer work. In 1977 production started to include gift-ware and writing desk items, and the first fountain pens were produced in 1982 for sale as proprietary brands by several well-known companies at the time. By 1989 pen manufacture had become the core activity of the parent company, Beta s.n.c., and in 1991 it decided to market its own fountain pens under the independent trademark Stipula.

Stipula was chosen as a symbolic trademark. In classical Roman times agreements were sealed by splitting a small piece

The Stipula 18c. gold nib.

COMPANY FACTS

EST. 1973

Florence, Italy

Impruneta, Italy

Specialist pen shops
Direct from Stipula
(BETA s.n.c.
Via Guido Rossa
14/16, Cascine del
Riccio, 50015
Impruneta, Firenze,
Italy.
Tel 055 209204)

$ ★ ★ to ★ ★ ★

ETRURIA

The oval Etruria was introduced in October 1995. It is available in two sizes, the larger being a piston filler and the smaller taking cartridges or a converter. It is accompanied by a rollerball, ballpoint, and pencil. It is made in either amber or black celluloid and the trim is solid gold and sterling silver.

FLORENTIA

The round Florentia range was introduced in October 1995. It is available in two sizes, the largest is a piston filler and the smaller accepts cartridges or a converter. It is accompanied by a rollerball, ballpoint, and pencil. It is made in either amber or black celluloid and the trim is solid gold and sterling silver.

NOVECENTO

The Novecento is made from flaming red ebonite with solid gold or silver trim. Stipula regard it as one of their most important lines as it combines tradition with modern restraint. It is available in two sizes, the larger is a piston filler and the smaller takes cartridges or a converter. It is accompanied by a rollerball, ballpoint, and pencil. A limited edition is also available in green-fringed ebonite.

IL DONO LIMITED EDITION

The Il Dono limited edition was released in January 1996. It is the first in a thematic collection on the values and symbols of Western civilization. The cap depicts the contest between Athena and Poseidon to decide which should be worshiped by the city of Athens and the fluted ebonite barrel is based upon the temple columns of classical Greece. The cap was designed and made by the Florentine master Paolo Cerrini using the traditional lost-wax technique; it is hand chiseled, signed, and numbered. The edition comprises 188 gold and 988 silver pens.

FLORENTIA

NOVECENTO

IL DONO LIMITED EDITION

of straw (*stipula*), and in modern Italian the word is still used for the formal act of underwriting an agreement. The company name is therefore a play on words, having the dual meaning of a commitment to produce a quality and reliable pen, and also stressing the personality and honor of an individual who makes an agreement.

Stipula refer to their working method as being like two souls. The lively "grandchild" is dynamic, using the most modern techniques, supervised by the wise and judicious "grandfather," who stresses the traditional and handmade elements. Their pens are state-of-the-art and are protected by modern patents, yet they are made from oldfashioned materials such as ebonite and celluloid which are then combined with traditional Florentine metalworking. Stipula's largest pens have their patented three-way filling system. As with other pens these can be filled with either cartridge or converter. But remove these and the whole barrel can become the reservoir, filled by a pump. The pens are hand turned from solid blocks of celluloid or hard rubber, the precious metal trim is always cast and set by hand. Traditional engraving and guilloche techniques are used to finish it.

An ebonite Etruria fountain pen in its
oval presentation box.

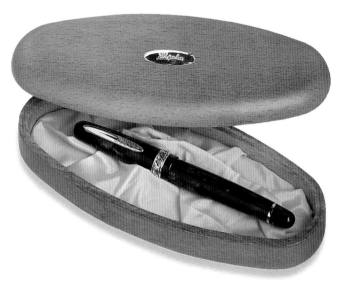

Florentia Aurea and Etruria Aurea. The Aurea range are luxury version of the Florentia and Etruria Pens having precious metal caps in 18-ct., 9-ct. gold or solid silver. Each piece is individually numbered.

COMPANY PRODUCTS

Known for luxury pens and regular lines

ETRURIA AND FLORENTIA
AUREA
NOVECENTO
IL DONO
VARIOUS LIMITED EDITIONS

NIBS: standard range

Visconti

Visconti was founded in 1988 and seeks to become the Rolls Royce of the pen industry. It was founded by Dante Del Vecchio and Luigi Poli who decided to form their own pen company, and their hobby became their business. The company

was named Visconti in honor of the Viscount who owns the Tuscan villa which is their main office.

Visconti's big break came with the discovery of a stock of old celluloid. Del Vecchio and Poli collected vintage celluloid pens, and were delighted to be able to start making them for themselves. They claim to be the first company to reintroduce celluloid pens, and since then many other companies have followed suit or tried to copy the celluloid effect.

Dante Del Vecchio researched celluloid material and processes, and the company acquired an enormous amount of technical knowledge in a short space of time. He is responsible for product development, and owns more than ten patents. Luigi Poli runs Visconti's marketing. In 1992 a chance meeting between Visconti and two American collectors Ed Fingerman and Jon Messer occurred at a vintage fountain pen show in Florence, leaving the Americans with the feeling that they had discovered a well-kept secret. Writing Design Inc. was

---

COMPANY PRODUCTS

Known for handmade luxury pens, and a wide range of accessories and collectors' pens, custom pens

VOYAGER
MANHATTAN
ALHAMBRA
PONTEVECCHIO
RAGTIME
VARIOUS LIMITED EDITIONS

NIBS: fine, medium, broad

INKS: wide range of inks and cartridges

VOYAGER

MANHATTAN

VOYAGER

The Voyager is Visconti's top-of-the-range pen. It was introduced in fall 1993 and comes in coral red or lapis-blue celluloid. In addition to the large pen Visconti produce a companion which can take rollerball, ballpen, or fiber-tip refills.

MANHATTAN

The Manhattan is one of Visconti's most popular pens. Production commenced in 1994 and the stepped ends are reminiscent of the Manhattan skyline where Fingerman and Messer had their offices. The celluloid also echoes the 1930s and recalls the Parker Vacumatic, which dominated that decade. In common with the famous Parker, the translucent hoops allow you to see how much ink remains in the reservoir. The collection comprises fountain pen and a convertible companion. Both are available in three colors, ruby red, emerald green, and sapphire blue.

*Luigi Poli with an array of laminated
sheets of celluloid.*

established by Fingerman and Messer soon afterwards to serve
as the North American distributor of Visconti.

Visconti has not resurrected an old pen; their designs are
unique. The feel and materials used are derived from the golden
age of the pen during the 1920s and 1930s, but the technology
and style is extremely modern. Visconti has been responsible for
several new developments, in particular a power filling system
introduced in 1993 which allows the reservoir to hold more ink
than six ink cartridges. In 1994 an ink shut-off double reservoir
allowed capacity to be increased to more than ten cartridges,
and also prevented the pen from leaking on airplanes. Visconti
are also very proud of their Traveling Ink Pot (1996) which is
made in several sizes to fit most brands' top-range pens so that
they can be filled anywhere at any time.

A pen takes about eight months to produce as celluloid needs
time to mature. Pens are turned from rods the diameter of the
barrel, or rolled from laminated sheets. Each pen is almost
entirely made by hand as celluloid cannot be injection-molded.

COMPANY FACTS

Est. 1988

Florence, Italy

Florence, Italy

Nearly worldwide, through specialist agents
New pens are announced in *Pen World* and collectors' magazines

$ ★ ★ to ★ ★ ★ ★

Polishing, turning, drilling, assembly, and trim-fitting are carried out by hand in the traditional way. There are 11 separate designs at the in-house planning prototype stages and these are due to be launched between the present time and the year 2001.

Visconti have achieved so much in such a short time because they offer a unique product; their pen is both pioneering and conservative and handmade to the highest possible standard. It is a big pen and appeals to businessmen and professionals, many of whom buy each model Visconti release. Visconti pens are a popular choice and their rare pens are already trading at premium prices. The consensus of opinion is that Visconti will be the company to watch in the future.

Each pen is hand-assembled in the traditional way. Here the nib is being secured.

MICHELANGELO

The Michelangelo limited edition of 1475 pens is the first in a series commemorating great artists. It was unveiled in 1995 and is available in two sizes. The Continental has a matte clip, the Oversize a polished clip and clear ink window. The pen is made in a variegated green-bronze celluloid and is accompanied by a matching traveling ink pot.

ALHAMBRA

The Alhambra is Visconti's most ambitious pen, launched in 1995. It uses a new proprietary process to embed, not just apply, precious metal into the surface of the pen and is also the first pen since the 1920s to be made in red hard rubber. The design is inspired by the Moorish muqarnas (honeycomb motif) which is found extensively in the Alhambra Palace, Spain— often regarded as the eighth Wonder of the World. It is offered as a limited edition of 888 pens in .999 fine-silver filigree, and a special reserve of 288 pens in 18-ct. gold filigree, with the trim in matching precious metal.

PONTEVECCHIO

The Pontevecchio is named after Visconti's hometown and has an outline of the famous bridge engraved on the band. It was introduced in 1996 and is available as fountain pen, rollerball, ballpen, and pencil in three striking new celluloids — Adriatic stone, Pompeii blue, and silver granite.

RAGTIME II

Ragtime II (or "new" Ragtime) is the latest version of one of Visconti's earlier models, and is a considerably expanded collection. The pen uses a piston filling system and is more slender than Visconti's premium models. It is accompanied by a matching ballpen and pencil and comes in a range of four colors.

ALHAMBRA

PONTEVECCHIO

RAGTIME II

Wahl-Eversharp

W AHL-EVERSHARP, like Lazarus, has returned from the dead and production of a new version of its most famous pen was resumed in France in 1996. The original Wahl-Eversharp company produced some of the most glorious vintage pens, but enjoyed a checkered history of corporate mergers from its inception and suffered at the hands of its own ballpoint.

The Ever-sharp pencil was invented in Japan by Tokuji Hayakawa and first imported to the United States in 1914 with enormous success. In 1915 Eversharp was bought out by the Wahl Adding Machine Co. of Illinois who were looking to expand into other fields. Wahl took over the Boston Fountain Pen Co. in 1917, marketing the first Wahl "Tempoint" pens the following year. In 1919 the adding machine division was sold in order that production could concentrate on pens and propeling pencils. Wahl's metal pens and pencils were launched in 1921 and were extremely popular.

In 1929 Wahl-Eversharp made a late entry into the celluloid pen market with their Gold Seal series of personal point pens. These had an easily interchangeable threaded nib unit and were extraordinarily popular. Moony's industrial manual shows that Wahl's net sales for this year rocketed to $5,697,938, more than twenty-five percent greater than the giant Parker Pen Company's. From here on it was downhill all the way and despite launching two pens which are highly collectable today, the Doric and the Coronet, sales slumped until Wahl merged with its subsidiary Eversharp Inc. in May 1940.

The new company responded with the launch of their best-selling pen, the Skyline. It was designed by Henry Dreyfuss

---

COMPANY PRODUCTS

Known for mid-price and budget pens, inks, and cartridges

SKYLINE SERIES

NIBS: three: fine 0.65mm, medium 0.8mm, broad 0.9mm

(1904–1972), the famous early industrial designer. He is renowned for work which includes the Bell cradle telephone, the Hoover vacuum cleaner with built-in lighting as well as the Hudson J-3 locomotive for the New York Central line, and airplane interiors. The Skyline had a striking tapered cylindrical shape and was extremely well-designed. It did not leak at high altitudes (due to a breather tube) which earned it the honor of being chosen by the American armed forces for supply to U.S. airforce pilots. Commercially Wahl-Eversharp took a huge risk, the development cost $237,000, but the resulting sales were spectacular in 1941, and had doubled by 1942.

Terminal decline started in 1945–46 when the C.A. (capillary action) ballpoint was launched. It was one of the first commercially-produced ballpoints after the war and seems to have been rushed into production, as by 1947 thousands were being returned under guarantee.

COMPANY FACTS	
Est.	1912–1917
🏢	Le Montlouis, 72510 Pontvallain, France
🏭	France
🚚	Best apply to headquarters
$	★

"Yellow Cab" is a special edition of the Skyline packaged with a taxi cab in a gift box. It is made in both fountain pen and rollerball.

Wahl-Eversharp staggered on until its writing instrument division was sold to Parker in 1957. Some unusual pens exist bearing both Parker and Eversharp imprints from the 1957–1961 period, but the brand was knocked on the head in 1961 due to unprofitable performance.

In 1995 the company was revived by Emmanuel Caltagirone in France who has had experience marketing other collectable pens. Caltagirone decided that the Skyline should be recreated as is because its distinctive silhouette would evoke strong brand recognition in a collectors' market which had seen the value of the original Skyline rise by almost five hundred percent in the mid 1990s.

There are plans for a limited edition of the Skyline Army pen. However, a large supply of aluminum needs to be found first. Currently Wahl Eversharp are looking for an early fighter plane in the desert frontier of New Mexico and Arizona to reclaim its aluminum. A total of 230 lb is needed for the first batch.

SKYLINE

The new Skyline retains the familiar sleek streamlined appearance and wrapover military clip. There are also modern features; a two-color rhodium-plated gold nib, and an interchangeable piston-cartridge filling system (the 1940s version was a lever-filler). It is made as a fountain pen or rollerball and is available in the following finishes; burgundy, blue and black with either silver- or gold-plated caps, blue with silver cap, burgundy or green with gold-plated cap. The nib is 18-ct. gold and follows the interchangeable personal point system of the 1929 Wahl.

SKYLINE DEMONSTRATOR

A poster from December, 1925, which advertises the latest line of ladies' pens.

SKYLINE DEMONSTRATOR

The Skyline Demonstrator is available as part of the Story collection. Transparent demonstration pens were originally made for salesmen, but soon achieved popularity among collectors who appreciated their rarity. They are now made as novel lines and sold directly into the retail market.

Waterman

WATERMAN HAVE BEEN MAKING PENS for longer than any other manufacturer, and are still one of the "big three" companies alongside Parker and Montblanc.

There is a well-known fairytale which relates how Lewis Edson Waterman, a New York insurance salesman, lost an important sale when his pen leaked ink over the contract. By the time he had another drawn up a rival had stolen his business. To prevent this happening again Waterman "invented" the modern fountain pen, making a new ink feed with a pocket knife, saw, and file, and using his kitchen table as his factory.

Lewis Edson Waterman, founder of the company, and reputed inventor of the modern pen.

This is a romanticized version of the truth, probably devised by L.E. Waterman himself. True, Waterman had been a struggling insurance salesman, but he had also been in the pen business long before his famous "invention." He had seen the potential of the fountain pen and opened a business at 136 Fulton Street in New York City during 1883. Waterman assembled pens from parts supplied by local jobbers, and then sold them himself. He formed the Ideal Pen Company with Asa Shipman, his best customer, in 1884—but the partnership dissolved leaving Waterman in control of their premises at 10 Murray Street even before his memorable first patent was granted on November 4th, 1884. Waterman had great faith in his product and was the first to offer a five year guarantee, and to use extensive and aggressive advertising to sell his pen as the best. This contributed to the steady growth of his company which had sold around 200 pens in 1884, 500 in 1885, and by 1900 was selling 1,000 a day.

Waterman was to remain a prominent force for the next three decades. The Heath firm of jewelers in New Jersey was employed to make precious metal and filigree overlays for Waterman's pens in an enormous range of styles. Unlike Parker however, who continued to use Heath for some time, Water-

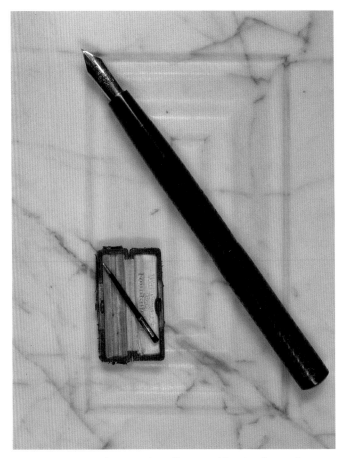

Waterman's largest and smallest pens. The giant #20 and the matchstick-sized Doll pen, both c.1910.

man was quick to develop his own in-house jewelers and produced a number of unique designs. They also offered a wide range of top quality hard-rubber pens from the matchstick-sized "world's smallest pen" to a giant #20 which were featured prominently in the firm's advertising and window displays. The firm used several filling mechanisms including eye-dropper and safety retractable pens. When the competition started to manufacture self-filling pens with an internal rubber sac, Waterman experimented with pump, sleeve, and coin-fillers before settling on a lever filling system (not unlike Sheaffer's) in 1915.

The creation of reliable export agencies around the world was critical in transforming Waterman into the first truly international pen company. An in-house publication *The Pen Prophet* was used to explain to sales staff the current range, advertising campaigns, sales techniques, and company news. At the time it contributed in no uncertain way to Waterman's success and today the few surviving copies are an incredibly important documentary source for the company's history.

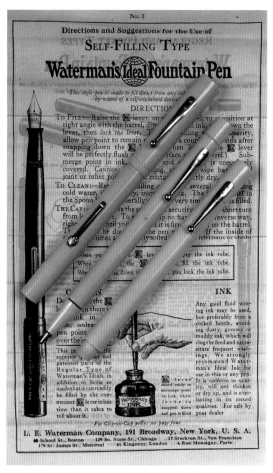

This very rare white celluloid doctor's trio of pen, pencil, and thermometer case made c.1927 is just one example of Waterman's versatile production at the height of their fame.

LADY AGATHSE

LADY AGATHE

A very clever design, produced with the lady's handbag in mind. It comes with its own container made from matching celluloid, and has a protective top for the prevention of leakage.

COMPANY PRODUCTS

Known for a full range of quality pens at all prices

LADY AGATHE
MAN 100
L'ETHALON
PREFACE
EDSON
EXPERT

INKS: range

Waterman were slow to move away from hard rubber and onto the production of celluloid pens. While Parker, Sheaffer, and others heralded a craze for color, Waterman were producing two-color, rippled, hard-rubber pens. Waterman's first celluloid pen, the Patrician, was a big bulky pen and was made when streamlined pens were in fashion. Today it is seen as the ultimate Art Deco pen, but despite posthumous recognition more than half a century later, it failed to maintain Waterman as a dominant force in the market. The American company went into a terminal decline under unsuccessful management and manufacture ceased in the mid 1950s.

Production was continued by the Canadian, English, and French factories. Jif-Waterman, the French subsidiary, was to be the standard-bearer for Waterman through the difficult post-war years. They had started production during World War I, when America was cut-off from Europe and were by far the most innovative company manufacturing under the Waterman trademark, developing a popular cartridge pen in the 1930s, and later responding to the challenge of the ballpoint following World War II, with their successful Pantabille four-color ballpoint.

The CF cartridge pen was introduced in 1954 and its enormous success managed to keep Jif-Waterman afloat despite suffering from a balance-sheet deficit and a bureaucratic, top-heavy management similar to that which had caused the demise of Waterman America. In 1969 Francine Gomez, granddaughter of Jif's founder, Jules Fagard, succeeded to the reins of the company and revitalized it. This dynamic woman pruned waste from the corporate structure and introduced a design consultant to creat a chic image. Jif-Waterman became Waterman SA in 1971, regaining the American trademark and, within eighteen months, control of the Canadian, English, Commonwealth, and Asian trademarks followed. The company was quoted on the Paris Bourse in 1975, and a new range of pens was designed in association with Alain Carré. The most important of these was

The Pen Prophet, *Waterman's in-house publication. This issue illustrates a campaign for their rippled rubber pens. Despite great success they dated fast since most competitors were already using celluloid by this time.*

the Gentleman, and elements from many others feature in today's lines.

Waterman was taken over by Gillette in 1987, and is now part of their stationery products division alongside Parker, Papermate, and Liquid Paper and is once more enjoying a taste of the success during its golden age.

MAN 100

L'ETHALON

PREFACE

EDSON

MAN 100

The Man 100 was introduced in 1983 when Waterman took advantage of their centenary to offer a new large-size pen in direct competition to the Montblanc 149. It has since been offered in a variety of finishes and materials including various plastics, woods, and precious metals. The current range comprises fountain pen, pencil, ballpoint, and convertible rollerball/ballpoint/fibertip.

L'ETHALON

Newly-launched, this pen is proof that Waterman are working hard to produce innovative designs.

PREFACE

This is Waterman's current line, available in a number of colors and with a fashionable soft nib. It was designed to appeal to the younger market.

EDSON

Named after Lewis Edson Waterman, the Edson is Waterman's current top pen and has been made since 1992. Initial response was hesitant, but sales have picked up following both advertising, and more importantly, word of mouth recommendation. Its shape is unlike any other Waterman pen and it has a harder nib than other pens in the Waterman line. Fountain pen and ballpoint are available in blue or green and it is the only Waterman pen guaranteed not to leak on an airplane.

Yard-O-Led

YARD-O-LED IS A NAME THAT HAS TRADITIONALLY been associated with propeling pencils, and has only recently expanded its range to include fountain pens under its own name. The Yard-O-Led pencil company was founded in 1934 by Leopold Frederick Brenner, a German working in the center of the London jewelry trade. Brenner was granted a patent on a mechanical pencil holding 12 leads 3" in length (collectively one yard) hence the name "Yard-O-Led."

Yard-O-Led's premises were demolished during the London Blitz in 1941, and after the war business was restarted by Brenner, with help from a new partner Frank Tufnell Jr. The firm set up a comprehensive range of first-class retail accounts including well-known stores like Asprey and Mappin & Webb and business prospered. Frank Tufnell Jr later purchased a majority shareholding in Yard-O-Led and also bought their main competitor the Edward Baker Company, who in their turn owned Sampson Mordan—the company who had perfected the first mechanical pencil in 1822—and for whom Frank Tufnell Sr. had worked before the war.

COMPANY FACTS	
EST.	1934
🏢	London, England
🏭	Hockley, Birmingham, England
🚚	Worldwide (part of Filofax group)
$	★ ★ to ★ ★ ★ ★

COMPANY PRODUCTS

Known for its regular line including pen, pencil, rollerball, ballpoint

VICTORIAN
PULLMAN AUTOMATIC
LIMITED EDITIONS

NIBS: fine, medium, broad, extra-fine available upon request

INKS: bottles, range of colors

IMPERIAL

PULLMAN AUTOMATIC PEN

IMPERIAL

Yard-O-Led's first limited edition pen of 1,000 pens. The choice of the Dragon, one of the most important symbols of Eastern legend and folklore shows how important the Far-Eastern market has become today. The Dragon is said to bring with it the four benedictions of the East; wealth, virtue, harmony, and long life.

PULLMAN AUTOMATIC PEN

Leopold Brenner was involved in Brenner-Pocock, one of whose products was the Pullman Automatic Pen. It is uncertain whether they were makers or distributors of this very rare vintage pen, which has been found around Europe marketed under a variety of names. Brenner is often found on the nib, but it is best known as the Pullman Automatic Pen. It was designed to be operated one-handed, the nib extending through a hinged cover as the end of the barrel was pushed into the pen. Boxes and instructions are very rare, and today the pen often sells for around $1,500.

*The Victorian emphasizes the connections of
Yard-O-Led with the nineteenth-century pencil industry.
The stylized floral design is used by no other
companies today.*

The factory moved from Augusta Street to larger premises near the jewelry center of Birmingham. The company was joined by Tim Tufnell who trained with a London manufacturing silversmith, and who today runs the business from within the Filofax group.

Yard-O-Led writing instruments are handcrafted in solid silver and gold based on traditional designs from the Victorian and Edwardian era. Each pen or pencil is handmade except for the mechanism, and it is the only remaining British pen company which still manufactures hand-crafted products to the same high standards established in the nineteenth century. Yard-O-Led writing implements are individually numbered on the clip, and available as standard in sterling silver, and 9-ct. and 18-ct. gold upon request.

Resource

Guide

Clubs and Magazines

THE REVIVAL OF INTEREST in fountain pens and fine writing over the last decade is reflected in the growing number of collectors' clubs and magazines around the world. The majority were founded through an interest in vintage fountain pens but now reflect the ever-larger proportions of their members or readers who use or collect modern pens. You will often read about a pen before it is launched if you take these club publications, and they are the best way to find out about pens sold only in a particular country or as very limited editions.

All the clubs and societies are very friendly and run by knowledgeable enthusiasts. Membership is usually inexpensive, often little more than the cost of printing and posting the club journal. Some, like the Pen Collectors of America, have a world-wide membership and a substantial reference library; membership is essential for anybody interested in vintage fountain pens. This is by no means a definitive list, rather the best-known organizations and those with an international profile. There are countless other clubs, societies, and magazines and you will usually be able to find something in most countries, although often hard to find and sometimes of a transient nature.

BENELUX

Benelux Pen Collectors' Association

c/o Marc Van der Stricht
Avenue Beau-Sejour 65
B-1180 Brussels
Belgium

Tel: (322) 374 0876

Publishes: *La Plume d'Oie/De Gazepen* quarterly

FRANCE

Plumes magazine

Outstanding glossy magazine published by Orlowski Editions in Paris. Available from newspaper shops or by subscription (*Plumes*/Orlowski 3 rue St. Philippe de Roule 75008 Paris). Essentially a lifestyle publication built around writing in all its forms, a typical issue will range from the latest fountain pens and chic writing accessories, through postal art to informed features on paper-making. Essential reading.

Club des Collectionneurs de Plumes

Boîte Postale 16
92312 Sèvres Cedex
France

Publishes: *Au Fil de La Plume* quarterly

GERMANY

Pen Plus magazine

The first issue of this glossy German language magazine was launched at the time of writing this book. It is *"dedicated to the antique pen as well as the new one …"* and *…"talking about the surrounding aspects, the lifestyle around the writing."* Editor: Tom Westerich, Pen Plus, Goller Verlag GmbH, Postfach 240, Hauptstrasse 4, D-76482 Baden-Baden, Germany.

F.S.D. (Fountain Pen Society of Germany)

c/o Stefan Wallrafen
Hinter den Wiesen 25
51105 Cologne 91
Germany

Organizes: pen shows in Cologne and Tilburg

Internationales Forum Historische Burowelt

c/o Prof. Dr. Gerd Krumreich
Im Grund 58 Dw-4W
D-4000 Düsseldorf 30
Germany

Publishes: *HBw Aktuell* quarterly

ITALY

Accademia Italiana della Penna Stilografica

Viale Dei Garibaldini 64
58035 Braccagni – GR
Italy

Contact: Letizia Jacopini
Tel: (564) 329672 and (0348) 2624797
Fax: (564) 39672 and (337) 714754

Publishes: *Stilomania*—quarterly Italian-language magazine. An excellent publication from a society which has worked exceptionally hard to offer an unrivaled service to its members. *Stilomania* is a blend of information about the booming

Plumes

Stilomania

Pen Plus

Italian pen industry, original research into vintage pens, listings, and reviews.

The Accademia also organizes pen shows regularly in one of Italy's many historic towns and cities.

Club Internazionale Della Stilografica

Via del Fonditore 10
Bologna
Italy

President: Raffaella Simoni Malaguti

UNITED KINGDOM

The Writing Equipment Society

c/o Mrs Maureen Greenland
Cartledge Cottage
Cartledge Lane
Holmesfield
Derbyshire
S18 5SB
U.K.

Organizes: regular meetings

Publishes: *W.E.S. Journal* quarterly

A society which represents a very diverse range of interests in historic writing equipment. The *Journal* publishes a great deal of original research unavailable elsewhere, usually about British companies. The WES also organizes book discounts for its members on many of the range of publications now in print.

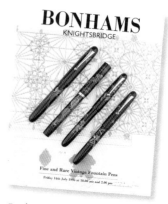

Bonhams

Bonhams Auctioneers

Montpelier Street
Knightsbridge
London SW7 1HH

Tel: (171) 393 3900
Fax: (171) 393 3905
Internet:
http://www.Bonhams.com
E-mail: dj11@cityscape.co.uk.

Expert: Alexander Crum Ewing

Not strictly a club or a society, Bonhams pioneered auctions of vintage fountain pens in the late 1980s and has remained undisputed world leader in this field ever since. Auctions are held five or six times a year in London, and a series of auctions in Singapore began in 1995. Their lavish illustrated catalogs are available either individually or by subscription and form an encyclopedic pictorial library of the world's rarest pens and price trends. This is usually the place to find rare limited editions which have sold out worldwide. Essential.

UNITED STATES OF AMERICA

The Pen Collectors of America, inc.

PO Box 821449
Houston
Texas
TX 77282–1449

Tel: (713) 496 2290
Fax: (713) 496 2290
Internet: 103352.3537
@compuserve.com

Members organize and attend the numerous pen-shows in the United States. The PCA grew from the Southern California club and has inherited and expanded their magnificent reference library of archive material and research, and photocopies are available by post to members.

Publishes: *The PENnant* three–four times a year. The world's leading publication on vintage pen tips and topics

Pen World

continues to receive and print new information on the hobby not yet available in the mountain of books on pen collecting. It is a useful forum for keeping up with pen news around the world and carries news of new lines as they are launched. Essential.

Pen World International

The leading English-language glossy magazine for pens. Now published bi-monthly and available from newspaper shops or by subscription from World Publications, 3946 Glade Valley, Kingwood, Texas 77339. *Pen World* has been criticized by established collectors for moving away from vintage pens toward a celebrity/lifestyle/modern-pen magazine. These observations are true, but it still sells in ever-increasing quantities and a German-language edition is now published. Vital reading to keep up with new pens as they are made around the world. Almost indispensible.

THE PENANT

Where to Buy Fountain Pens

I N MANY COUNTRIES you will be able to find a reasonable selection of fountain pens in major department stores and high street stationers. The last decade has also seen an increase in the number of boutiques for several international luxury brands, where you will find a full range of their products. However the independent specialist pen retailer often reigns supreme with the very latest products, the widest range of pens and accessories, and will also provide a personal service and impartial advice. This is a guide to some of the most interesting ones in the major cities of the world.

BELGIUM
Lipajou
5 place des Tilleuls
5004 Bouge

Pen & Pencil
Melkmarket 35
2000 Antwerp

CANADA
Winston & Holmes
138 Cumberland St
Toronto
Tel: (1) 416 968 1290

FRANCE
Cartier S.A.
13 rue de la Paix
Paris

Dubois
24 bis, rue Soufflot
Paris VM

Montblanc
60 rue du Faubourg
St-Honore
Paris VIIeme

Mora
7, rue de Tournon
Paris Vleme
Tel: (331) 43 54 99 19

Point Plume
21 Rue Quentin
Bauchart
75008 Paris
Tel: (331) 49 52 09 89

GERMANY
Dorrbecker
Sogestrasse 36/38
28195 Bremen
Tel: (49) 421 308
0842

Thessinger
Steinwegpassage 7
60313 Frankfurt
Tel: (49) 69 28 1339

The Writing Gallery
Eichhornstrasse 13
1/2

97070 Wurzburg
Tel: (49) 931 544 42

Ulrich Krüner
Jenaer Strasse 15
10717 Berlin
Tel: (49) 30 853 3644

Versand Historischer
Schreibgeräte
Firma R Martini
Birkerfeld 16
51429 Bergisch
Gladbach
Tel: (49) 2204 85509

GREECE
A D Evangelidis Ltd
15 Spiromiliou
Arcade
10564 Athens
Tel: (30) 1 322 8825

HONG KONG
Exclusive Trading
Company
4/F, 17D Nassau St
Mei Foo Sun Chen
Kowloon
Tel: (852) 2742 5452

ITALY
A C Vecchietti
Via Manzoni, 6
Bologna
Tel: (39) 51 22 39 51

Antica Cartoleria
Novocento
Piazza Risorgimento
3
Milano
Tel: (39) 2 76 00 61
23

Bravaccini E Ronconi
Viale dei Mille, 30
Cervia
Tel: (39) 544 97 30 36

Brunori Stilografiche
Via Torino 77
Milano

Tel: (39) 2 86 45 18
21

Cartablu
Via Roma 84
Salerno
Tel: (39) 89 23 66 70

Cartoleria Abc
Via Jesolo, 56
San Dona di Piave
(VE)

Cartoleria Rossi
Via D. Fermelli, 12
Mantova
Tel: (39) 32 05 26

Cartoleria Signorelli
Via D. Fiasella, 14/R
Genova
Tel: (39) 10 58 16 69

De Santis
Via Scarlatti, 177
Napoli
Tel: (30) 81 55 60 922

Ditta Pineider
Piazza della Signoria
13–12
50122 Firenze
Tel: (39) 55 28 46 55

E E Ercolessi
Corso Vittorio
Emanuele, 15
Milano
Tel: (39) 2 76 00 00
74

Il Calamaio
Via Livornese, 325
Lastra a Signa (FI)
Tel: (39) 55 87 22 137

La Boutique Della
Penna
Via Cavour 142
Asti
Tel: (39) 141 50 090

La Boutique Della
Penna
Coros Umberto 1,
108–110

Napoli
Tel: (39) 81 55 45 067

La Nuova Stilografica
Corso della
Republica, 165
Forli
Tel: (39) 543 20 171

Maria Lazzaroni
Via Calatafimi 2
25122 Brescia
Tel: (39) 30 37 53 184

Mazza Stilografiche
Via Cesare Canti 3
Milano
Tel: (39) 2 86 46 11
31

Moscetti E C
Corso Garibaldi, 43
Cremona
Tel: (39) 372 20 24 05

Oldrini Cancelleria
Corso Garibaldi, 113
Legnano
Tel: (39) 331 54 03 43

P. C. di Russo e C.
Largo Vasto a Chiaia,
86
Napoli
Tel: (39) 81 41 87 24

Penne D'Epoca
Largo Castello, 4
Ferrara
Tel: (39) 532 21 00 91

Regali Novelli
Via S. Marcello, 39
Roma
Tel: (39) 6 67 92 852

Stilofetti
Via degli Orfani 82
Roma
Tel: (39) 6 67 89 662

JAPAN
Hakase
605, Sakae-cho
Tottori-City
Tel: (82) 22 3630

LUXEMBOURG
La Civette
22 b rue de la Porte
Neuve
2227 Luxembourg

NETHERLANDS
P W Akkerman
Passage 15
2511 Ab Den Haag
Tel: (31) 70 346 2264
Fax: (31) 70 363 3551

NEW ZEALAND
Europens
Level 3
Atrium On Elliott
Auckland

PORTUGAL
Papelaria Progresso
RUA. Do Ouro
Lisbon
Tel: (351) 1 342 2181

SINGAPORE
Ngee Ann City
Montblanc
Boutique
391 Orchard Road
#01-32 Ngee Ann
City
Tel: (65) 735 5038

Raffles City
Montblanc
Boutique
250 North Bridge
Road
#02–03 Raffles City
Shopping Centre
Tel: (65) 334 1903

Seiju Wing On
Department Store
230 Victoria Street
Bugis Junction
Tel: (65) 223 2222
Ext. 851

SPAIN
Central de la
Estolgrafica
Barcelona

SWITZERLAND
Naville
Rue du Mont Blanc
1211 Geneva

UNITED KINGDOM
Battersea Pen Home
PO Box 4361
London SW11 4XP
Tel: (44) 171 652 4695

Cartier
175-176 New Bond
Street

London W1Y 0QA
Tel: (44) 171 493
6962

City Organiser
40 Bow Lane
London EC4M 9DT
Tel: (44) 171 248
8326

City Organiser
15 Cabot Square
Canary Wharf
London E14 1XX
Tel: (44) 171 628
6585

City Organiser
14 Turl Street
Oxford
Tel: (44) 1865 792327

Classic Pens Limited
PO Box 826
Epping
Essex CM16 6DT
Tel: (44) 1992 524444

Mallins Just Write
25 Martineaux
Square
Birmingham B2 4UB
Tel: (44) 121 236
1410

Pencraft
119 Regent Street
London W1R 7AH
Tel: (44) 171 734
4928

Pencraft
27 Royal Exchange
London EC3V 3LP
Tel: (44) 171 626
4679

Penfriend
Bush House Arcade
Bush House
Strand
London WC2B 4PH
Tel: (44) 171 836
9809

Penfriend
34 Burlington Arcade
Piccadilly
London W1V 9AD
Tel: (44) 171 499
6337

Pens Plus
70 High Street
Oxford
Tel: (44) 1865 241174

Signatures
20 Backswinegate
York
Yorkshire
Tel: (44) 1904 631311

The Edinburgh Pen
Shop

63 Thistle Street
Edinburgh EH2 1DY

Woods
12 Old Bond Street
Bath
Tel: (44) 1225 445347

UNITED STATES
Arthur Brown & Co,
Inc
2 West 46th Street
New York
NY 10036
Tel: (1) 212 575 5555

Artlite
1851 Piedmount Rd
NE
Atlanta
GA 30324
Tel: (1) 404 875 7271

B Collins Limited
318 S Dearbon St
Chicago
IL 60604
Tel: (1) 800 404 PENS

Berliner Pen
928 Broadway
Suite 805
New York
NY 10010
Tel: (1) 212 614 3020

Broomfield Pen Shop
5 Broomfield Street
Boston
MA 02108
Tel: (1) 617 482 9053

Cartier Inc
653 Fifth Avenue
New York
NY 1002

Chicago Gold Inc
1150 N State St.
Suite 300
Chicago
IL 60610
Tel: (1) 312 440 1303

Copelin's Office
Supply Center
425 West Main
Norman
Oklahoma 73069
Tel: (1) 405 364 7011

DA DA
500 Pacific Avenue
San Francisco
CA 94133
Tel: (1) 415 623 2520

Daly's Pen Shop
Crown Center
Kansas City
Missouri
Tel: (1) 816 474 7500

Daly's Pen Shop
275 W. Wisconsin
Ave

Milwaukee
Wisconsin
Tel: (1) 414 276 8900

Fahrney's Pens
8329 Old Marlboro
Pike,
B-13
Upper Marlboro,
MD 20772
Tel: (1) 301 568 6550

Fahrney's
1430 G Street, NW
Washington D.C.
Tel: (1) 800-624 7367

Fountain Pen
Hospital
10 Warren Street
New York
NY 10007
Tel: (1) 212 964 0580

Gilbertson &
Clybourne
Marriot Hotel
Chicago
Illinois

Joon Stationery
782 Lexington
Avenue
New York
NY 10021
Tel: (1) 212 935 1007

Menash Signatures
213 West 79th Street
New York
NY 10024
Tel: (1) 212 595 6161

Pen & Pad
8204-A Menaul NE
Albuqueruque
NM 87110
Tel: (1) 800 717 PENS

Rebecca Moss
510 Madison Avenue
New York
NY 10021
Tel: (1) 212 935 1007

Seattle Pen
1424 4th AVE
Suite 527
Seattle
Washington
Tel: (1) 206 682 2640

The Fountain Pen
Shop Inc
510 West 6th Street
Suite 1032
Los Angeles,
CA 90014
Tel: (1) 213 891 1581

Venture
1156 Madison Ave
New York
NY 10028
Tel: (1) 888 388 2727

Index

Picture Credits

The Publisher would like to
thank all individual
companies for contributing to
this title, and for sending
items or photography.
Additional pictures were
supplied by the following:

Alfred Dunhill pp45, 46, 49,
53; Aurora pp5, 55, 57, 61–64;
Bonhams, London pp9, 10,
13, 16(b), 31, 41, 50, 51, 52,
54, 72, 100, 144, 173, 175;
Bonhams – Gerald Sattin
Collection pp 14, 15(r), 16(t),
20, 21, 22, 23(l), Bonhams
Parker Collection pp30, 32,
34(l), 35, 40; Caran D'Ache
p68; Cartier pp76–77; A. T.
Cross pp86–90; Alexander
Crum Ewing pp12, 15(l,c),
18(t); Diplomat pp91, 93(r);
CM Dixon p 7; S. T. Dupont
pp96–97; Faber Castell p103;
Hakase pp109–111; Hulton
Getty p34(r); Journal of the
Royal Society of Arts No.
2763, 3rd November, 1905
pp23(r), 26; Lamy pp112–114;
Herve Obligi p128;
Montblanc pp2, 125
(Montblanc Collection), and
pp33(r), 119, 122 (The Art of
Writing); Parker pp39,
129–140 (Parker Heritage);
Platinum pp142–143; Recife
pp146–148; Sheaffer pp43,
153, 156, 158; Stipula pp159,
163; Visconti pp 36, 166, 167;
Waterman p174.